DOUBLE BIND

DOUBLE BIND

ESCAPING THE CONTRADICTORY
DEMANDS OF MANHOOD

RODNEY L. COOPER, PH.D.

ZondervanPublishingHouse
Grand Rapids, Michigan

A Division of HarperCollinsPublishers

Double Bind
Copyright © 1996 by Rod Cooper

Requests for information should be addressed to:

📖 ZondervanPublishingHouse
Grand Rapids, Michigan 49530

Library of Congress Cataloging-in-Publication-Data

Cooper, Rod, 1953–
    Double bind : escaping the contradictory demands of manhood / Rodney L. Cooper.
      p.   cm.
    ISBN 0-310-20324-4 (alk. paper)
    1. Men (Christian theology)   2. Men—Religious life.   3. Double bind (Psychology)
    I. Title.
    BT703.5.C66   1996
    248.8'42—dc20   96-12535
                                                                                                              CIP

International Trade Paper Edition 0-310-20834-3

This edition printed on acid-free paper and meets the American National Standards Institute Z39.48 standard.

Edited by Ed van der Maas
Interior design by Sherri L. Hoffman

Published in association with the literary agency of Wolgemuth and Hyatt.

Printed in the United States of America

96 97 98 99 00 01 02 /❖ DH/ 10 9 8 7 6 5 4 3 2 1

Contents

CHAPTER 1

Double Trouble

Once a young man named Joe attended a professional truck driving school. There he learned such basics as how to back the long trailers up to a loading dock with pinpoint precision and what gear to use when going down different grades of incline. After passing his driver's test, however, he also had to pass an oral exam as part of his graduation requirements.

The instructor posed certain hypothetical situations to Joe and asked how he would handle each one. One of the questions the instructor asked was: "Now, Joe, you've just peaked the top of a mountain with a full load, and you're now descending at about fifty-five miles per hour. You see a gentle curve up ahead, and you know that to take it safely you have to put on the brakes. But, Joe, you discover you don't have any brakes, so you barely make it around the curve. Now you're going sixty-five to seventy miles per hour, and you know you have to slow this rig down, so you reach for the emergency brake and pull with all you have, only to find that you don't have an emergency brake anymore either. You are now going eighty to ninety, and you have to slow this rig down somehow, so you look for an open space you can pull off into. But Joe, you can't do that because you have two ninety-foot gullies on each side of you. And to top it all off, Joe, you are now going a hundred miles per hour, and right at the bottom of the mountain is a freight train stopped and loaded down. Now, Joe, what are you going to do? How are you going to get out of this?"

Joe thought for a minute and then responded, "I'd wake up John who's sleeping in the back."

"Why would you wake up John?" the instructor asked.

"Because he's *never* seen a wreck like this one before!"

———◦———

Joe was put into an impossible situation. No matter where he turned he was hemmed in. His only recourse was to brace himself for the crash.

Many men in our society feel just like Joe. They look around and see very few, if any, options and feel they are racing toward calamity, and many of them, like John sleeping in the back, have chosen to ignore their circumstances until a major crisis, such as divorce or loss of health or job, wakes them from their sleep.

Why do men feel such stress? Why are they so frustrated just being men? Why do they seem numb to the potential destruction of their own physical well-being and that of their families?

I believe that men do not know who they are as men. Rather they define themselves by what they do, who they know, and what they own. Men are looking inside and not finding much, if anything, to hold on to.

Did you catch it? The reason men are so "bound up" is because they *do not know who they are*—it's an *identity* problem.

If the major issue affecting men is their identity, then how does not knowing who you are affect you physically, spiritually, emotionally, and relationally? What are some of the factors that have caused this "Joe-like" dilemma?

I have found from working with thousands of men that they are hurting—badly. I believe men are hurting because of a false belief system.

MACHO-MACHO MAN

The false belief system that keeps men bound is the persistent belief in the "Male Mystique." This myth defines men in our society as successful only if they exhibit four key characteristics:

1. *Autonomy.* As men, we are to be completely independent. We are to personify the slogan I saw on a T-shirt the other day that said, "A man's gotta do what a man's gotta do"—kind of a "Rambo" mentality. As a result, we are separated from any kind of real community. It is our job to be depended upon, but we must not depend on anyone. Asking for help is a "no-no." Even with a simple task, such as asking for directions, a man would rather be lost for three hours than be dependent and ask. Of course, you know why they are now sending women astronauts on missions—because now someone will at least be there to ask for directions. (Sorry, I couldn't help it.)

2. *Efficiency.* We are to be productive and effective. We must work harder—not smarter.

3. *Intense self-interest.* We must be goal oriented, and nothing must get in our way. One executive put it well when he said, "If your family keeps you from getting to the top—then get a new family."

4. *Disconnectedness and emotionlessness.* We must be able to block out emotions because they keep us from being focused. If a man is emotional he may end up not reaching his goal.

Marvin Allen, Director of the Texan Men's Institute says, "Society requires men to live in a box labeled MAN. Scrawled on the outside of the MAN box are dozens of rules: 'Compete,' 'Succeed,' 'Perform,' 'Don't feel,' 'Don't revel any weaknesses,' 'Get a grip,' 'Tough it out,' 'Ignore your physical symptoms,' 'Win at all costs,' 'Have all of the answers,' 'Fix the problem.'"[1]

I am not saying that these characteristics, in and of themselves, are bad. In our society many of these are needed for a man to survive. But that's the problem. Men are rewarded for suppressing their emotions, which are required for relationships. In exchange for the privilege of "making it" on their own, men are taught to repress many of the emotions that might expose their vulnerability.

Historically, men were not always expected to achieve everything alone. Men worked the land and helped each other in a community setting. I grew up on a farm and oftentimes, I would go with my father to raise a neighbor's barn or help him bale hay. When lunchtime rolled around, there would be fifteen to twenty of us men eating, drinking, and sweating together. There was a sense of community.

Today, that is not the case. We have moved to a more "every man for himself" mentality. The new male mystique teaches that the successful man is to be competitive, uncaring, and unloving. We, as men, are not to connect to one another because we are in competition with one another. The masculine code may make him a deadly fighter; it may grant status and power; it may push him higher up the ladder, but in exchange, the man gives up his compassion, empathy, sensitivity, and joy. It decreases the pleasure he finds in his daily life and keeps him isolated and alone from his family; and he has no friends—only acquaintances. It is not by accident that the second leading group of people, after teenagers, to commit suicide are men seventy years of age or older. Why? Because they look around and find themselves all alone.

But I believe that the greatest contributors of men being in the sad predicament we face, more than the male mystique, are the "double binds" we face.

ALL BOUND UP AND NOWHERE TO GO

Writer Sam Keen and Dr. Ofer Zur wanted to find what men and women thought were the characteristics of the ideal man as well as the inferior man. They wanted to know which people, either living or dead, would seem to fit those criteria. So Keen and Zur developed a questionnaire that first appeared in *Psychology Today*, March 1989. The magazine soon received and analyzed more than six thousand replies.[2]

I will not go into all the results, but I will list the characteristics of the ideal man. According to the survey, the ideal man is receptive, responsive to the initiative of others, strong, intellectual, moral, he pays attention to diet, exercises, is healthy, expresses feelings of sadness, stops often to wonder and appreciate and dream, follows inner authority, is even-tempered, moderate, easy to be with, nonjudgmental, willingly accepts help, he is a doer, and takes charge.

The characteristics of an inferior man are: he ignores his body, never shows pain, has mood swings, is critical, introverted, always where the action is, a type A personality, suave, and urbane.

The authors of the study then asked the men and women respondents to name two people as most embodying the ideal, good, average, and inferior man. The following lists will show who men and women chose respectively:

IDEAL MEN

Women said:	*Men said:*
Jesus	Jesus
Ghandi	Ghandi
Tom Selleck	John F. Kennedy
Abraham Lincoln	Abraham Lincoln
Paul Newman	Martin Luther King Jr.
Martin Luther King Jr.	Thomas Jefferson
Bill Cosby	Winston Churchill
John F. Kennedy	George Bush
George Bush	Billy Graham

What makes these men ideal? Each one was perceived as being caring/loving, intelligent, moral/honest, sensitive, and a family man.

Some of the inferior men mentioned are as follows:

INFERIOR MEN

Women said:	*Men said:*
Adolf Hitler	Adolf Hitler
Ayatollah Khomeni	Ayatollah Khomeni
Donald Trump	Donald Trump

Charles Manson   Charles Manson
Archie Bunker   Archie Bunker
Mike Tyson   Mike Tyson

————◦————

What makes them inferior? Each was perceived as egocentric, immoral, violent, greedy, insensitive to others, bigoted, and stupid.

I find it interesting that in this secular survey, Jesus was picked as number one by men and women. It shows that our Lord Jesus is recognized for his solid character and moral integrity—an ideal man looks like Jesus.

You might ask, "So what?" Don't miss what I am about to say: in our society, these ideal traits—sensitivity, taking care of one's body, listening, and showing emotion—are actually those that often make it impossible for a man to "make it" in our culture. Such a man might actually be perceived as inferior. The men who get ahead—who are our culture's success stories—are often those who ignore their bodies, do not show pain, have type A personalities, and so on. This is a "double bind." A man is told he should be one way, but he is also told that he should be the opposite to succeed. A double bind is a no-win, damned-if-you-do-and-damned-if-you-don't situation. And we all experience them.

Men find themselves in many double binds. We are caught between what we as boys were taught was masculine and what is now expected of us as adults. We are torn between our inner needs and the denial of those needs due to social pressure. We are constantly dealing with contradictory demands that psychologically, emotionally, spiritually, and physically fragment us.

For survival's sake, we are forced to function in a machinelike, emotionally detached way—in other words, with the traditional male façade: cool, detached, controlled, guarded, and disengaged. We end up responding to external cues like a programmed computer, rather than wrestling with life's ambiguities and tensions. We find ourselves having no passion or joy.

After a while, we either become passive or aggressive—angry all of the time.

I know what I am talking about—I was one of the aggressive ones. One day while mowing the lawn, I was having trouble with my mower. I had not used it for a while, so I cleaned the spark plug, changed the oil, and tightened the belt. I pulled on the cord several times but the engine would not turn over. Finally, after about ten tries, the mower started. I took a step when the mower—you guessed it— died on me. I tried two or three more times, but it would not cooperate. All of a sudden, I felt something I had not felt in a long time. Not anger—it was more than anger—it was rage. I started kicking the mower, then lifted it up over my head and threw it into my neighbor's yard! When I came to my senses, I looked next to where I threw the mower, and there was my neighbor—in shock. I said to him, "Happy Birthday, I hope you enjoy the mower." He was speechless. About ten minutes later, I sheepishly walked to his house and asked him for my mower back.

Why did I feel such rage? Why was I so out of control? Why did I have this gnawing feeling inside of me? Could it be because the double binds finally caught up with me? Yes, I believe so.

I Don't Get No Respect

In Aesop's fables there is a story about some frogs who wanted a king. They pestered Jupiter so much that he finally tossed a log into the pond. For a while the frogs were happy. Soon, however, they discovered that they could jump up and down on the leader, run all over him, and he offered no resistance, not even a response. Not only that, but he had no direction or purpose; he just floated back and forth on the pond.

This exasperated the frogs. So, back to Jupiter they went, insisting that they be given a strong leader. Jupiter, weary of their complaints, sent them a stork who stood tall above the frogs and certainly had the appearance of a noble leader. The frogs were happy. Their leader stalked about the pond making great noises and attracting great

attention. The frogs' joy, however, soon turned to sorrow and ultimately panic when the stork king began to eat his subjects.

This fable describes the dilemma of what it means to be a man in
today's society. On the one hand, men are either numb and passive,
like the log, or they are angry and aggressive, consuming everyone
around them, like the stork. In my counseling I have observed that
men usually go to one extreme or the other out of exasperation.

As I conduct leadership seminars for Promise Keepers, I hear two
laments: the first is "I'm damned if I do and I'm damned if I don't."
Men tell me they feel caught in a meat grinder and cannot win no
matter what they do.

The second lament is "I don't get any respect"—the "Rodney
Dangerfield Syndrome." Today, men in our culture are often seen as
incompetent or unnecessary. Dr. Gary Oliver says that "men have
become the dumb blondes of the nineties." If we were to base our view
of men on such women's magazines as *Redbook*, *Cosmopolitan*, and
Good Housekeeping, we would have to conclude that men cannot love
or experience closeness, they are either sexually demanding, clumsy,
disinterested, or unable to consider a woman's sexual needs, and continually trying to escape from relationships.

The electronic media does not paint men in a very pretty light
either. Aside from reruns of *The Bill Cosby Show*, try to think of one
television show on which men are viewed positively. Men are usually
seen in the light of Homer Simpson on *The Simpsons*, or Al Bundy on
Married with Children. Rarely does a man seem to be in charge or
know what he is doing. Usually the children or the wife save the day.

Let me give you some examples. Budweiser used to produce a
series of commercials with the tag line "Why ask Why?" One in particular comes to mind. In it, a woman goes out on dates with four different men. The first night she goes out with a man dressed in a blue
three-piece suit with a nice power tie. His demeanor is businesslike.
Suddenly, in the midst of their lovely evening, a phone rings. He
reaches into his inside suit pocket and pulls out a cellular phone. He
says to the woman, "Wait a minute, I have to make this deal." The
second night the woman goes out with a man who looks like he has

stepped off the front cover of *GQ*. He is wearing an exquisite Italian silk suit with a beautiful flowered tie. Every hair is in place, every muscle toned, and he is tan all over. He looks at his date and says, "Some women find my looks intimidating." The third evening she goes out with a man in army camouflage pants, a green sleeveless vest, dog tags around his neck, and a scraggly beard and disheveled hair. He sits backward on the chair and says with a wild-eyed look, "And there I was, there I was, there I was in the Congo." Finally, on her fourth date, she goes out with a guy in faded blue jeans and a white T-shirt. A pack of cigarettes is rolled up in his sleeve, and he is wearing cowboy boots. He has a wad of chew in his jaw, and looking at her plate, he notices she has not eaten all her steak. So, reaching with his fork, he drags it over to his plate saying, "Sweet thing, you weren't going to eat that were you?" and proceeds to polish off her steak.

This commercial is obviously humorous, but notice what it says about men. The first man, with his cellular phone, shows us a workaholic who cannot relax. The second man, who is caught up in his own looks, portrays men as self-centered and egotistical. The third man, who talks about his exotic adventures, is seen as "the little boy who never grew up" and cannot make a commitment. Finally, the fourth man is the "macho" man who must always be in control. Yet, what is truly sad is that the commercial goes on and says, "But, you can always count on Budweiser for that crisp, clean, clear taste time after time." The commercial ends up implying that their beer can be counted on because it is consistent—unlike men who cannot be counted on and are not consistent.

A recent article in *Newsweek* documents a major shift in advertising depicting men as, get this, "The Ad World's New Bimbos."

In another commercial (for a computer) two men and a woman are caught in a traffic jam. The two businessmen in the back of the vehicle are in a panic about their inability to get needed materials for a presentation to their partner who is already at the meeting site. They begin to say, "Game over—game over, man. We have lost the account." Without batting an eyelash, the woman in front pulls out her cellular phone, plugs it into the computer, and coolly and calmly faxes the needed materials to their partner who is at the site. The two men in the back relax and say, "Where do you want to have dinner?" The woman ends up saving the day. It seems that the media has taken great delight in portraying men as not being able to rise to the occasion when a crisis occurs.

I was home one afternoon working on a presentation when I decided to take a break and watch television. I channel-surfed for a while until I came across *The Oprah Winfrey Show*. On this particular day, her show was entitled, "Successful Women Who Have Made It In a Man's World" (or something like that). One comment, which got a round of applause, appalled me. A single woman said she was glad there were sperm banks because, while she wanted to be a mother, she did not want the hassle of having a man around to raise the child. In essence, men only got in the way and gummed up the works.

The complaints about men, the idea that they are jerks, have become vital advertisers. After analyzing a thousand commercials in 1987, researcher Fred Hayward found that when an advertisement called for a negative portrayal in a male-female interaction, an astonishing 100 percent of the time the "bad guy" was the man.[3]

Not only does television portray men in a bad light but most of the literature on male-female relationships points out how, for the most part, women have to deal with a man's severe problems. A sampling of the cards in the "Love and Relationship" section of a card store reveals a heavy antimale bias. Hold onto your hat as you read some of these titles: "If they can send one man to the moon, why can't they send them all?" "When you unzip a man's pants . . . his brains fall out." And finally, "If we can make penicillin out of moldy cheese, maybe we can make men out of the lowlifes in this town."

Or read some of the book titles on relationships in your local bookstore. Aaron Kipnis, in his book *Knights Without Armor*, has done a masterful parody of the titles concerning men:

> We have *Smart Women, Foolish Choices* and *Women Who Love to Much*. There are *Wild Women and Passive Men* and women with the *Cinderella Complex*, who find *No Good Men* while facing the *Don Juan Dilemma* in relationships with men who have the *Peter*

Pan Complex or the *Casanova Complex.* They wonder *Should Women Stay with Men who Stray, Men Who Can't Love,* or *Men Who Cannot Be Faithful?* There are also *Men Who Hate Women and the Women Who Marry Them,* who have given rise to the *Men Who Hate Themselves and the Women Who Agree With Them.*[4]

There are also "dumb men" joke books. Let me give you a sampling: "Do you know the difference between government bonds and men? Government bonds mature." "What is the difference between E.T. and men? E.T. phoned home." And "Why is psychoanalysis a lot quicker for a man? When it is time for him to go back to his childhood, he is already there." The list just keeps going. And what do all of these titles have in common? Men are the ones who have most of the problems.

Finally, one of the most popular TV shows is *Home Improvement* with Tim Allen. Even there, the man is often out-smarted by his wife and children. What makes the show so delightful is that Tim is willing to learn even though he goofs up—a lot.

No wonder that, on top of suffering from the Macho-Macho male image, men feel they get little respect or support.

Does all this make you feel trapped? Often angry? I'll bet you long to be free. Well, I have some good news for you. There is an answer. You can escape the double binds. In the following chapters, we will define each of the double binds men face, and I will offer suggestions on how to escape it.

There is one double bind, however, that if escaped will unlock the door to freedom from all the others. What is this powerful double bind? How does one begin to escape? Read on, my brother, help is on the way.

DISCUSSION QUESTIONS

1. What messages about men have you observed from the media? Give some examples. Are they mostly positive or negative?

2. What is the hardest thing about being a man? What do you resent? What difficulties, injuries, and pains have you suffered because you are a man?
3. Does your personal style fit the description of the stork or the log? Why or why not?
4. Read Romans 12:1–2. How do these verses affect a man's perspective on his culture?

Chapter 2

Escape to Freedom

Let me tell you a story about a little black boy who, when he was ten, went on a march with his Boy Scout troop. The scout leader said that their reward at the end of the march would be to go to a swimming pool where there were slides and rides. After the march, all of the boys put on their swimsuits and lined up at the gate to pay their three-dollar entrance fee. When it was the boy's turn to pay, the attendant stopped him: "Son, are you black or do you just have a good tan?" He could not tell, you see, because the boy happened to be light-skinned. The attendant said, "Since I'm not sure, you will not be allowed to swim here today. This is a *private* pool."

Although the scout leader suggested that the boy might want to hike back alone and get a special merit badge for his effort, the rest of the boys in the scout troop declared that if *he* did not swim, then neither would they. The boys saved the day, and they all ended up at a public beach.

My friend never forgot that incident. It contributed to his growing up believing that being black was probably more of a handicap than an asset, and he concluded that if he was going to make it, that he would have to perform better than everyone else—just to compensate for his blackness.

So he became good—real good. He played the trumpet and became the number one trumpeter in Ohio. He graduated in the top five of his class. He went to college and, once again, was at the top of his field. Still, there was an uneasiness about him because he was constantly trying to deny a part of himself. He performed well, but he could not get too close to anyone because they might reject him for being black. He also became quite angry because he felt so all alone. He was a black man trying to make it in a white world.

Finally, he thought that going to seminary would change all that. He would now be around believers. But the sting of prejudice found him there too, since he was one of only three blacks on campus. He performed well and won the preaching award, but he walked around alone and angry.

Then one day he moved to Houston, Texas, to begin his first ministry. There, by "accident," he met a white man by the name of Bill, the pastor of a growing church. There was something different about Bill—he was real and open and talked freely about his many struggles and victories.

He invited the black man over to his house one day, and soon they began spending every Tuesday together. They became soul mates. In their time together, Bill could see my friend's struggle—his performance mentality he had so that he could cover up his blackness. Bill took a risk and shared openly about how he admired that part of his friend.

Then one day it happened. Bill invited my friend to come to his church and preach. After the sermon and they were at his home for dinner, Bill sat me down—yes, I'm really talking about myself—and Bill put his hands on my shoulders, looked me straight in the eyes, and said, "Rod, I thank God for your blackness. It's not a handicap. God didn't make a mistake. Thank him right now for all of who you are—your blackness included."

I struggled and squirmed, and then I broke into tears. "Thank you, Jesus, for making me who I am—for making all of me." I stood up, and we hugged and cried, as I finally felt accepted for all of me—all of who I am.

Then Bill said he loved me.

I looked at him, and then I said, "I love you too, man."

Proverbs 18:24 says, "There is a friend who sticks closer than a brother." Bill was that friend—he was truly my "soul brother."

Bill gave me a priceless gift that day. He helped me come to grips with an issue that keeps most men hamstrung in relationships and from having the intimacy they long for. What is that issue? Simply put—from where do I get my identity? For men, I have found, identity precedes intimacy. It is very difficult for me to give security and affection to those around me if I am uncertain about who I am. It is my belief the Identity Double Bind is the key issue a man must settle if he is going to be free in all of the other areas of life.

The Identity Double Bind

It goes like this: at work, a man is often success and achievement oriented, so that he develops a style of being dominant, aggressive, emotionally detached, and controlled. At home with his family, however, he is expected to be tender, empathic, sensitive, selfless, warm, and caring.

Either Way He Loses

If he tries to be a whole person he will either be too soft at work or too harsh at home. If he tries to be all things to all people, the aggressor at work and the lover at home, he ends up splitting his personality. His life becomes a series of performances. He passes or fails depending on who he is with at the moment.

John was a classic example. Slender, grayed-haired, in his late fifties, he was a top executive and lived in the most exclusive part of the city. He had a distinguished air. Yet one day he just decided to walk out of his marriage of thirty-five years. He took a leave of absence from his job and moved into his own apartment. His wife, daughter, and company colleagues were shocked and bewildered. They could not understand this sudden change of behavior. They begged him to get counseling, which is where I came into the picture, because John was a member of the church where I was the pastor of counseling.

John walked in and sat down in the chair across from mine. His steel-blue eyes peered at me, and then he exploded in anger. "I am not going to take it anymore."

"Take what?" I asked.

"Living life by everybody else's expectations," he replied. "I have tried to be a good husband and father. But whenever I feel we have arrived, my wife announces that we 'need' so much more. So I go after it for her and the kids. But I never hear that it is good enough—there is always more. It is the same at work. I meet the standards but then we get an announcement from the board that we must do better. Rod, when is enough enough? I do not have the energy for this anymore. I have no idea who I am. I fear retirement because I have no idea what to do—where to go. You see, I am the go-to guy for everybody else. I feel like a tire with a slow leak. The air has been going out of my life over the years, and I just woke up and found that my life, like the tire, is flat. I figure if I just leave and start over now I might have some time left to find myself." John then broke down in tears.

Herb Goldberg, in his book *The New Male*, accurately sums up John's position by saying, "It has become increasingly clear that the gender orientation known as masculinity has serious and troubling limitations and, consequently, has put the male clearly in crisis. . . . He possesses little insight into the causes of what is happening to him and has few inner resources to draw on for nourishment during the difficult times. He is truly a cardboard Goliath, unable to flow self-caringly with the changing social scene."[1]

Men like John look inside and find nothing to hold onto for stability because they have let others define their identity. Approval becomes the all-consuming passion in their life. That is why men desperately try to define themselves by three things:

• What they do

- Who they know
- What they own

These three elements give them the sense that there is a payoff for giving up bits and pieces of themselves along the way. Positions and possessions become symbols of how it is worth sacrificing myself—who I am—in order to have these wonderful things. The problem is that the older one gets, the bigger the payoff has to be. I call this "feeding the machine."

Research has shown that men, more than ever, want to have loving, solid relationships with their families and their God. In a word, men want to experience intimacy. Intimacy is the ability to experience an open, supportive, compassionate relationship with another person without the fear of condemnation or losing one's identity in the process. Intimacy is also the sharing of the soul—hopes, dreams, fears, shames, and sorrows. Intimacy is knowing another person deeply and well—and appreciating him or her anyway. It is an easy, comfortable balance between dependence upon another, and independence—the living of one's own life; of aloneness and sharedness; of distance and closeness. This is what I experience still from my friend Bill, and this is what John longed for in his life, and, ultimately, was able to achieve.

The kind of pain, isolation, and performance orientation that I described above is not unique to me or John. I see it in a lot of men. I see a yearning for intimate relationships. But if men want truly intimate relationships—and intimacy depends on how secure a man is in his identity—then where do they get their identity? Where does it all begin?

FATHER KNOWS BEST

Research shows that men are taught not to give each other affection. A father stops hugging his son somewhere before the boy reaches his teens. From then on, no other man seems to touch the boy much except to give him a firm handshake. Affection is assigned to only the emotional and sexual sphere of life, therefore it becomes reserved for women. The only way a boy knows he is affirmed by his father is through the way he performs.

It is my belief that every boy wants to know that he is okay with his dad. Every boy wants to know that he has received a paternal blessing. If he doesn't receive it, then he will go through his whole life trying to get the approval he missed.

How important is the blessing? In the Old Testament a man could not lead his family or live his life without receiving the blessing from his father. The father would "lay hands on" the son as a way of giving him approval for who the son was and not for what he had done. The blessing bestowed favor upon that son so that he could feel, tangibly, the support of the one bestowing the blessing. It was a way to enable a son to fulfill his calling and purpose in life.

Even Jesus, before he embarked in the ministry, received a blessing from his Father. Matthew 3:13–17 describes how Jesus was baptized by John the Baptist, and upon coming out of the water, as the Scripture says, "Heaven was opened, and he saw the Spirit of God descending like a dove and lighting on him. And a voice from heaven said, 'This is my Son, whom I love; with him I am well pleased.'" The Father touched him with the Spirit in order to empower his Son.

So too every man needs the approval of his father to fulfill the calling God has given to him. If he doesn't get it he feels cheated. Let me give you an example.

You remember the story in Genesis of Esau and Jacob, in which Esau lost his birthright and also his father's blessing. You would expect that Esau's grief would be for the lost inheritance because his father, Isaac, was very wealthy, and as the eldest son, Esau should have inherited all of his wealth. But notice chapter 27, verses 34 and 36: "When Esau heard his father's words, he burst out with a loud and bitter cry and said to his father, 'Bless me—me too, my father. . . . Haven't you reserved any blessing for me?'" What really devastated Esau was not the loss of the inheritance, but the loss of the blessing from his father. He could not truly fulfill his calling without that blessing. As men, we have a tremendous God-given need to be blessed and affirmed so that we can make an impact on our world.

I was very fortunate. My dad gave me the blessing. My father's touch made a difference in my life. I called him Mr. 5 x 5 (because he was as broad as he was tall). He was five-foot, ten inches tall and weighed 260 pounds. He had twenty-two-inch biceps when he was seventy years old—a Caleb in the flesh. He could pick up 250-pound tractor weights in each hand and toss them where he desired. I respected that man—and I didn't want one of those arms getting loose on me!

My mother tells me that when I was six months old, my father used to take me to the feed store in the truck. He often changed my diapers along the way. The men in the feed store then asked him what he had in his hands—"feed," he said, holding up one hand. "Boy," he said, holding up the other.

As I grew up, whenever we finished planting a field, he would say to me, "Now, son, let's kneel and pray and ask God's blessing." He would pray and I would pray. Later, when the harvest came due, he would say, "Son, let's rejoice—God has answered our prayers."

But what I remember most is when I was twenty-one, and I came home from college. No sooner had I stepped out of the car than he gave me a bear hug, kissed me on the cheek, looked me straight in the eyes, and said, "Man, it's good to have you home, son—I have missed my boy."

Gentlemen, what do you think that did for me? I got the blessing! I knew I was valued for who I was—not for what I did. Research shows that warm, nurturing fathers do not create effeminate sons but men who are not afraid of intimacy. Men who know who they are as men.

But not all blessings are as good as the one my father gave me. There are many faulty blessings that can actually exacerbate the problem of a performance mentality.

Fathers can pass on a "performance mentality" to their sons in several ways:

1. *A "Spotlight Blessing."* This happens when only one person in a family receives the blessing. The other members must then "compete" to try to take the blessing away from the one who has favor. Joseph and his brothers are a classic example. If you remember, Joseph wore a many-colored coat, which was usually given to the oldest son, indicating that he was the next in line for the inheritance. In this case, Jacob gave the coat to Joseph, who happened to be the next to the youngest. Not only did this break tradition but it was seen as an insult to Joseph's brothers. In essence, Jacob was saying that the rest of his

sons were not worthy to have the coat. It also set up tremendous sibling rivalry, to the point that the brothers sold Joseph into slavery. Such are the effects of a spotlight blessing.

2. *"Never good enough."* This is where the blessing is always kept just out of reach. The high jump bar is always set a little higher once the person has cleared it. Many fathers do this to their sons. For instance, one young man from Dallas, Texas, heard that he just received a full-ride scholarship in engineering to Southern Methodist University. He went to his father with this news, thinking he would be praised for his efforts. His father coolly put down the paper he was reading and said, "Well, son, you know that the best engineering schools are in the Northeast." His son was crushed and two days later tried to commit suicide. One more time he had come up short. It really hurts when your best is not good enough. But a man learns early that "what he does" is more important than "who he is," so he starts to perform.

A man then learns that performance is how to get the blessing—he hopes. The following diagram shows how we try to compensate for that lack of the blessing.

How does man naturally try to build self-worth?

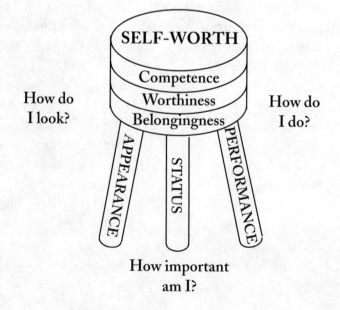

How do
I look?

How do
I do?

How important
am I?

FRESH STARTS

If a man does not receive the blessing from his father—the blessing that is essential for a man's identity—then how does he start over?

A new blessing begins by realizing that our heavenly Father has also given us the blessing through his Son Jesus Christ. I no longer have to seek human approval because I, as a son of God, am approved by the One who matters most—God himself. My identity is no longer based upon what I do, who I know, or what I own—but now is based upon *whose* I am. I no longer have anything to prove.

God values me as his child for three reasons, none of which are based upon performance.

First, he made me the way I am. Psalm 139:13–16 says:

> For you created my inmost being;
> you knit me together in my mother's womb.
> I praise you because I am fearfully and wonderfully made;
> your works are wonderful,
> I know that full well.
> My frame was not hidden from you
> when I was made in the secret place.
> When I was woven together in the depths of the earth,
> your eyes saw my unformed body.
> All the days ordained for me
> were written in your book
> before one of them came to be.

When was the last time you looked in the mirror and said, "Man, what a miraculous creation of God I am!" David says God looks at you and says that very thing. Think about it. God put more than 9000 taste buds on your tongue. God put more than 200 bones in your body. God put more than 600 muscles on those bones. God put more than 107,000,000 cells in each of your eyes. God put more than 60,000 miles of arteries and veins in your body. God even knows the number of hairs on your head (which, in my case, since I am follicly impaired, would not take long to count!). God made you the way you are and he loves it.

The second reason you will always be valued by God, apart from your performance, is that he paid a significant price to have a relationship with you. John 3:16 says that "God so loved the world that he gave his one and only Son that whoever works hard enough to earn his favor will be saved." I am sorry, that was a slip of the pen (or computer). No it says, that ". . . whoever *believes* in him shall not perish but have eternal life."

There is a story about a woman who loved to watch the Oakland A's back when Catfish Hunter was pitching for them. She would drive two hundred miles to watch them play. One day, after making the long trek, she was cheering for Catfish from the bleachers, but in about the fifth inning, Catfish began to walk batters and give up runs. The woman stood up and yelled with her husky voice, "Catfish, I want you to know that I did not come all the way down here just to watch you lose." Apparently he heard her and went on to win the game.

My friend, Jesus did not come all the way down to earth just to watch you lose either! He came to bless you and bestow favor upon you so you can truly be all that he has created you to be.

The third reason the Father values you apart from your performance is that he is committed to making you look like his Son, Jesus Christ. Romans 8:28–29 says, "We know that in all things God works for the good of those who love him, who have been called according to his purpose. For those God foreknew he also predestined to be conformed to the likeness of his Son." The word "good" here means that which conforms us "to the likeness of his Son." There is no wasted experience in a believer's life because God is using it all to make us look like Jesus. There is no such thing as a failure in the Christian life—God is using those circumstances to strip away everything that would hinder us from looking like him.

Once there was a young man who worked in a gold-processing plant with an older, more experienced man. The young man was just learning the process and said to the old man, "Today, let me tell you when the gold is ready to be poured."

The old man said, "Okay."

The young man came back after two hours and said the gold was ready. The old man shook his head and said, "No, not yet."

The young man came back after three more hours and proclaimed the gold was ready to pour. The old man shook his head once again and declared, "No, not yet."

Two more hours passed, and the young man said, "The gold has got to be ready now."

The old man said to his apprentice, "Come with me." They walked over to the big black pot with the boiling gold in it. The old man said, "Son, do you see all that dirt coming off of the gold?" The young man nodded. The old man said, "We call that dross—we don't want that in the gold. Do you know how to tell when the gold is ready to be poured into bars?" The young man shook his head with a no. The old man said, "When you can look into the gold, and see only the reflection of your face."

Take heart, my friend, because God uses every trial you face to get rid of the dross in your life so that when you face your next trial, all you and others will see as you handle it will be the reflection of his face. God wants Jesus to shine through you in every trial.

Now you might say, "Well, Rod, this is all fine and good, but so what? How does this really make a difference in the way I live? How does this get me out of the performance trap?" Let's look again at another diagram to see how we have changed.

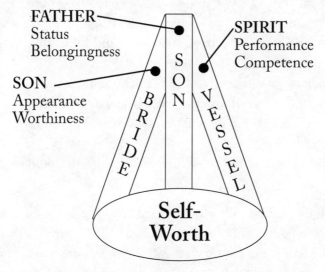

HOW GOD EXPERIENCES ME

The diagram shows that I no longer have to "do to be"—I do because I am. This frees me up because I have received the blessing to be just what God wants me to be.

Let me demonstrate it just a little differently by asking you a question: if Jesus Christ were to walk into your church on Sunday morning, who would he most want to sit next to? Some of you might say, "Well, probably the pastor or one of our deacons or elders." Did it occur to you that he might want to sit next to you? You might wonder, "Well if he did sit next to me what would we talk about? I know a lot about fishing and about my kids and wife, but I wouldn't know what to say to Jesus. We could talk about the Scriptures, but this is Jesus after all. . . ."

Well, if Jesus were to walk into this room right now, he might say, "Yeah, there's the pastor and the deacons or elders but I want to sit next to *you*." He might start the conversation by saying, "I understand you like to fish—tell me about the biggest fish you caught, and I'll tell you how I made it." Jesus would probably go on to say, "Tell me how the wife and the kids are doing." You see, Jesus is interested in you.

Some of you may be saying, "Well, I know he wouldn't talk to me, because I struggle with pornography" or "I am having a hard time controlling my temper." I have good news. I believe Jesus would sit next to you and say, "Hey, I understand you're struggling. Tell me about it—I want to help you through the struggle. I have a whole book filled with people who have struggled, and look what I did for them! I can do it for you too."

When a man sees himself as God sees him, he can live life at full throttle without the fear of disapproval. He can be himself because he has the blessing from the One who matters most. He can now be free from life's double binds.

David Needham, in his book *Birthright*, illustrates who we are in Christ this way:

> Imagine that you are a very typical boy in high school who likes two things most of all: food and girls (in either order). If someone asked you who you were and you were quite honest you

would have to express both your identity and your reason for living in those terms (with a long list of other ones of course).

One day you're standing by your locker in the hall and the track coach spots you. He takes you by surprise when he strolls purposefully over to your locker to talk to you ... "Say (says the coach) I have been watching you walk—gotta lot of bounce in your step. Whether you know it or not, you're a sprinter. With a little training you could be setting records in the 100 yard dash. I just know it."

"Aw, c'mon coach. I'm no sprinter. I might win a gold medal in eating or girl watching, but a sprinter? You have got to be kidding."

"No, I am not kidding. And I'll prove it to you. This afternoon—at practice." Now he has hooked you. You go to practice that afternoon ... and every afternoon for weeks to follow. You're first clockings aren't that outstanding but you sense a strange exhilaration as you run that maybe—just maybe—the coach was right. In the days that follow you read biographies of great sprinters; you watch films of great races. You run and run and run. It hurts so much sometimes, yet always deeper is a growing sense of identity. You are a sprinter. Before long the whole shape of your life bends to this new sense of personhood. If someone walks up to you on the street and asks "Who are you?" even before you can give your name you spontaneously respond ... "I'm a sprinter" ...

Saturday comes. The crowd stirs as you walk across the cinders to your starting block. Suddenly the prettiest girl from high school walks straight up to you with a large juicy piece of apple pie fresh from the oven and topped with a big glob of ice cream. She coos, "I brought this for you." Now comes the decision. You can do whatever you want. But what will you do? It all depends on your concept of those two words: *identity* and *meaning*.

Who are you? Are you a skin-wrapped package of taste buds, salivary glands and sex drives? If this is your identity then there isn't much question where you will find meaning. Or are you aware of something else? A new identity. An identity reinforced by warm relational times with your coach, by a new focus on personhood, a new set of values. If these things are true, your response to sweet Sue will be automatic—and conclusive. With scarcely a second look at her pretty face, you turn to focus on the tape 100 yards away. "Sorry Sue, I'm a sprinter. I don't want that apple pie (not simply I can't have it). Life for me is touching that tape before anyone else. What you offer just doesn't fit in. Thanks anyway."[2]

Let me tell you another story. Once there was a pudgy little boy who carried it with him when he entered high school. He literally was the "butt" of tons of fat jokes. He was five foot, eleven inches tall and weighed 250 pounds. People rejected his friendship time and again. He asked one of his female classmates out on a date, and she literally laughed at him when he asked her. The crowning blow was when he scraped up enough courage to go out for the football team. The coach told the team to run laps. The team finished far ahead of my friend and were doing their final push-ups by the time he made his last lap. When he started to do his push-ups the coach came up to him and said, "Son, don't bother. You're too fat to do anything. Just give it up." He walked off the field crushed.

In the midst of all of this rejection his parents and some friends kept loving him and telling him that Jesus loved him as well—just for who he was. One Sunday morning it was as if the preacher were talking just to him. He heard him say that there was a Friend who would "stick closer than a brother." He needed that kind of friend. One who would accept him no matter what, who would love him no matter what. He trusted Jesus that day for his salvation.

A major transformation took place in his life. There was a saying in his church about the wondrous changes that take place when Jesus enters a person's life: "When I got saved that's when my feet got a brand new walk and my speech got a brand new talk. I ain't what I ought to be, I ain't what I could be, but thank God I ain't what I used to be."

The boy changed—even physically. He felt that in order to be a good testimony for Jesus he needed to change his diet and lose some weight. He learned that self-control was a fruit of the spirit and asked the Lord to help him change. By working on the farm and fasting on a regular basis he shed sixty pounds that summer. He was now a mean, lean preaching machine.

Some of the other kids didn't even recognize him when he returned to school because he had changed so dramatically. The football coach even asked him if he would try out for football—but he lovingly declined. The girl who had rejected him the year before now wanted to go out. It was even sweeter to turn her down. He had a new-found confidence because he was no longer the same man—he was a new man. He was—well, he was a new me. I no longer saw my myself as a pudgy butt of jokes but now was a child of the King. I had full approval from the One who runs the universe. I now wanted to be my best self for him—not to be accepted—but because I was accepted.

You see, I now had *nothing to prove—nothing to hide—and nothing to lose* as my friend Ken Davis would say. Paul said it best when he said, "Therefore, if anyone is in Christ, he is a new creation; the old has gone, the new has come!" (2 Cor. 5:17). I now have a solid foundation in my house. Oh, I may have to do some remodeling along the way or remove or add a room. But essentially I am solid in my foundation. How does this make a difference? Let's look at the double binds in the following chapter and discuss the masculine straitjacket our society has placed upon men to see how being grounded in God frees us from these binds.

DISCUSSION QUESTIONS

1. "Men tend to define themselves by who they know, what they own, or what they do." Do you agree? Why or why not?
2. What is your primary source of identity? Who are you?
3. Did you receive the blessing from your dad? If so, when? If you have sons, have you given the blessing to them?
4. How does knowing who you are in Christ change your identity as a man? How does knowing you are a son of God free you up?

CHAPTER 3

A Man's Gotta Do What a Man's Gotta Do

One of the ways I keep up on what is happening around the world and in my local community is by reading the newspaper. I love to get up in the morning and sit down with a good cup of coffee and the newspaper. I must admit there is one section I always turn to first. No, not the sports page. I turn to the intellectual page, otherwise known as the comic strips. I love to read *The Far Side, Peanuts, BC,* and *Mother Goose and Grim.* One comic strip, *Sally Forth,* is especially interesting because it shows a career husband and wife who have one daughter. They seem to be the typical nineties couple struggling with the roles and the rigors of career, marriage, and family.

Recently they ran a series of panels about how Sally's husband, Ted, handled a male coworker who broke down and cried in the coffee room at work. The conversation went like this:

Sally: C'mon Ted. Tell me the rest of the story. Four or five of you were in the coffee room.

Ted: Yeah, and Ed started to ... um ... cry.

Sally: What did you do?

Ted: We walked away.

Sally: You just left him there?

Ted: C'mon Sal, a crying guy doesn't want an audience. We all went back to work and pretended we never saw a thing.

Sally: It's amazing you men aren't more messed up than you are. I can't believe one of your coworkers starts crying in the coffee room, and you guys just walk away.

Ted: What did you want me to do?

Sally: You could have put your arm around him.

Ted: A guy loses it at the office and another guy puts his arm around him? Give me a break.

Sally: He needed comforting.

Ted: So maybe we should have invited him for a beer after work.

Sally: I still can't believe it. Your workmate Ed was in the coffee room crying and you guys just walked away.

Ted: We thought he needed privacy.

Sally: You didn't even ask what was wrong.

Ted: I asked later.

Sally: Well at least there is hope.

Ted: I asked his secretary. [Sally drops her head] Now what?

Sally: So did you find out why Ed was crying at work?

Ted: His wife finally got pregnant with their first child and then miscarried last week. I guess Ed saw a baby picture on someone's desk and kind of lost it.

Sally: That's so sad. How can you even tell the story without choking up?

Ted: [He quickly starts to walk to the bathroom] I'll get you a Kleenex from the bathroom.

Sally: You'll have to blow softer than that, tough guy. I can hear you.

Sally: Well, no wonder Ed was crying. You didn't tell me his wife miscarried. Did you talk to him?

Ted: If I talk to him he will know I saw him crying.

Sally: So what?

Ted: He will be embarrassed. Besides, what would I say?

Sally: How about, "I heard about your loss, Ed. I want you to know how sorry I ..."

Ted: Wait, not so fast. [Ted is writing Sally's suggestion] "I heard about your ..."[1]

The conversation concerning Ted's coworker shows several key differences between men and women. Sally would have put her arm around the coworker, but Ted distanced himself. Sally would have asked what was the matter; Ted left him alone to deal with it by himself. Sally would have listened and shown empathy; Ted, not knowing what to say, didn't say anything; if they had had a couple of beers, then maybe they would have talked. This implies that it takes a drink or two to loosen a man up, before he can really start to feel.

Ted was not capable of giving his coworker those types of responses because at a certain age he was taught to turn them off. It is not that he is incapable of making those responses, but like a muscle, those feelings and responses have atrophied over time without use. Ted, like many men, is caught in the Gender Double Bind.

The Gender Double Bind

It goes like this: A young boy's most profound influences come from those who raise him: his mother, grandmother, and his teachers (who are usually women). From them he learns such traits as compassion, nurturing, kindness, and so on. Dad is in the background, often preoccupied and minimally involved. This goes on for about five years. Then, as if by magic, by the time the boy turns six he is expected to be "all boy." The solid traits he has learned from Mom are to be stuffed, for to express those traits or to behave in a feminine way makes the boy vulnerable to sarcasm from his dad and his peers. To survive, the boy must disown that part of himself that has been shaped by his mother. He usually does this by going to the opposite extreme.

Either Way He Loses

If he displays any "feminine" traits, he may be seen as soft or "wimpy," which will cause great anxiety and humiliation. When, on the other hand, he represses and denies the maternal traits he has learned, he lives as an incomplete person, alienated from that part of himself that is key for developing intimate relationships. He thus becomes a person who either needs to control others or who develops physical ailments as a result of "stuffing" a part of himself. He will adopt the creed: "A man's gotta do what a man's gotta do."

The age of five or six is key for a boy because that is when he begins to interact with other boys. To garner respect and have friends, he soon learns, he must not be like *girls*. I remember an incident in first grade that brought this fact home to me. While I was talking to one of my friends, another boy came up and began to put me down. I vividly recall him saying he did not like my jacket because it looked like something his sister would wear. I thought the best way to stay out of a fight was to ignore him. Wrong! He sucker punched me. While I was not looking, he hit me in the stomach as hard as he could. I immediately doubled over and found myself crying. The crying only lasted for a moment because all of my buddies were standing around to see how I would react. Instead, between huge gasps of air, I walked up to the guy who hit me and said, "It didn't hurt man—it didn't hurt," as I did everything I could not to break out crying. When the bell rang for recess to end, I acted like I needed to get something from behind a bush where I threw up and cried some more. I cried—but *they* (the guys) weren't going to see me cry. Even at six years of age it was important for me not to be seen as weak, needy, or in any way dependent because that would mean I was acting like a *girl*.

In our culture, girls, who later become women, are supposed to have the following characteristics: sensitivity, kindness, gentleness, love, meekness, thoughtfulness, compassion, tenderness, and the ability to nurture. Before age five or six many boys exhibit these traits, but when a boy starts school a new set of traits has to be developed. In fact, the boy is usually rewarded for suppressing those so-called feminine traits. He is now rewarded both by men and women when he displays such characteristics as toughness, aggressiveness, independence, competitiveness, being unemotional, rational, logical, and a host of others.

Research shows that when a child complains of a minor injury, parents are quicker to comfort girls than boys. Research also shows that since boys are considered emotionally tougher than girls, they are more often reprimanded in front of the class for misbehavior, whereas girls are more likely to be taken aside and spoken to more softly.

It has also been shown that *Dad*—not Mom—is the primary teacher of sex roles. Mom may be the earliest influence in the lives of both boys and girls, but later on Dad actually clarifies for both boys and girls what expected feminine and masculine behavior is. To illustrate, James Moore tells the following story:

> When I was about ten years old, my mother gave me a Ken doll for Christmas so I could play with my younger sisters and their Barbies. That, in itself, is a disturbing memory. But the part I remember most vividly was when my father came into the room and argued with my mother over giving me a doll. There I was, sitting on the living room floor playing dolls with my sisters, listening to my parents argue. Suddenly, my father looked at me with disgust and walked out of the room. I don't recall that any more was ever said about the Ken doll. I only know that those few minutes marked me indelibly with a sense of being a little guy who was somehow fundamentally defective. My father's expression had said it all.[2]

The identification process for boys and girls begins around school age. Research shows that both men and women reward or punish boys and girls according to how well they are exhibiting the appropriate characteristics for their gender. Both genders suffer as a result of having to possibly stuff certain parts of their personality because they do not fit the "man" or "woman" box.

BOYS TO MEN

Why does a boy learn to suppress these supposedly "feminine" characteristics? Because to fulfill the role of being a protector and a provider in this society, he must not let these softer characteristics get in the way. Our culture rightly maintains that men are more efficient workers and warriors when they are not inconvenienced by these softer characteristics.

Let me highlight how this carries over into adult life. In a research article "On Executive Suicide" in the *Harvard Business Review*, author Harry Levinson points out that when a highly successful man is at the end of his rope, he usually feels he cannot admit to having problems or needing help. To seek help from a friend or a doctor would be a sign of weakness and a failure to cope. Levinson's study further found that when the successful man seeks help from a psychiatrist or a psychologist, he fears being viewed as either weak or crazy or both.

After counseling hundreds of men, I am sad to say that the only time they come to see me is when they have already lost their job, wife, or health. When it's too late—then they come. Levinson's study also points out that a successful executive who refuses to seek help will then do one of three things: (1) He will develop psychosomatic illnesses like ulcers, heart problems, or severe back pain. (2) Or he will become hypercritical of himself and adopt a Nike Attitude—a "Just Do It" mentality—that eventually leads to severe burnout. (3) Or he will commit suicide.[3]

I know this is what happens because I saw it happen to the man who mattered most to me—my father. There is no question my father loved me. He was not afraid to hug me, kiss me, and tell me he loved me. I had the joy of knowing this man and feeling his love for me. I also saw him cry and express emotion. Now you might say, "Rod, this doesn't sound like the hardened executives in the study."

No, my dad had no trouble giving—he just had trouble asking for help. He was a proud man. He took seriously the admonition to provide and protect his family. Yet his concept of providing was to make sure Mom and I were taken care of—and no compromise. He was an excellent farmer. We had a 500-acre farm in Ohio where we raised a variety of crops and animals. We had 150 acres of corn, 200 acres of soybeans, 50 acres of wheat and the other 100 acres was grazing land for our beef and milk cows. We also raised about 1000 head of hogs. The "ham" business was our main source of income. My father was also "Farmer of the Year" in Ohio at one time. He was a good farmer.

But then we hit three bad years when the crops did not do so well and the stock prices for beef and pork fell. I remember my father sitting down and telling me about how "bummed out" he was. He told me how other farmers in the area were going into deep debt just to survive. I told him I would pray for him and that I loved him. I was a senior at Ohio State at the time.

The next Monday I called my father just to say hello. He sounded more cheerful and assured me that "everything was going to be all right." I told him I would see him that weekend after the football game, where I was to perform in the Ohio State Marching Band.

I will never forget what happened next. That Wednesday morning, I had just finished having my quiet time during which I had read the passage that talks about God's grace being sufficient for me (2 Corinthians 12:9). I said, "Lord, whatever happens today, I believe your grace is sufficient."

About five minutes later my mother called on the phone. "Rodney," she said. "You need to come home. Daddy is gone."

"What do you mean he's gone? Did he just leave?"

Mom said, "No, your daddy just decided it was time to go be with the Lord. He's gone."

"I'm on my way," I said.

I drove the sixty miles home at breakneck speed. When I walked into the house, my sister greeted me, and we both wept uncontrollably. The first question on my mind was why? I found out later that he had written a suicide note. I recall it saying, "Mama, call Mr. Jones, he will help you sell the equipment and the crops. Do not take a penny less than what the market will give. Also tell Ed [our hired hand] to sell the pigs for the market price. We can get it. Finally, tell Rodney I love him and that I just could not take it anymore. I believe that God's hand is upon him and *he* will truly take care of him. I love you, goodbye. Rodney."

I learned later in my counseling courses that the reason my father was so happy and lively on the Monday before his suicide was that he had made his decision. He had decided that if he committed suicide that we could sell everything and get out of debt. This was his way of providing. He saw no other way out. It would not have been manly to ask for help. He would never have asked me to quit school and go to work. This was his way of taking care of our family.

Let me tell you something. I wish my dad were here today. I would have loved for him to see me graduate from Ohio State, go on to get my Ph.D., and to meet my bride. They would have loved each other. I miss him and often wish I could ask his advice. But rather than asking for help, he sucked it up and did "what a man's gotta do."

If you are a man who has stuffed the softer side of who you are, then you are denying a part of yourself that is essential for the enjoyment of life. By putting yourself in the "man" box you end up cheating those around you out of what they desire most—you. All of you. Let me share with you two other consequences of stuffing the softer traits.

IRON BYRON

I love to play golf. There is nothing quite like the feeling of a 300-yard drive, right down the middle. I lack, though, what most weekend golfers lack—consistency. I often wish I were like "Iron Byron"—the machine used to test the distance capabilities of golf balls. You just set the amount of air pressure, push a button, and "pow," the ball takes off like a rocket. Just set the machine, and time after time, you get the same perfectly consistent swing.

Many men I work with act like Iron Byrons—like machines. They crank it out day after day after day. At lunch a friend of mine and I were talking about how much pressure we were under. He said, "Rod, I can't believe how stretched I feel. My kids want a piece of me, my wife wants a piece of me, my job wants *all* of me. I feel like a computer where you input certain commands and then I just go crank it out." Many men develop what I call a "Timex watch mentality"— they are supposed to "take a lickin' and keep on tickin'."

Yet even Iron Byrons fall apart. Another friend of mine, Jim Neal, told me that the company that makes the Iron Byron had one of their machines on display at a golf tournament. He said that after hitting the ball too many times, Iron Byron began to smoke so much that they had to shut it down. Its bearings had begun to wear out, and it was smoking because it was running out of oil and had started to lock up. Iron Byron needed an overhaul.

This happens to many men. For a while, most men—especially younger men—can simply gut it out through sheer determination. But the older a man gets, the less energy he has, and the more he begins to smoke (get angry) because he is slowly losing the oil of joy in life.

One of the results of becoming a "machine" and losing energy is a loss of *spontaneity*. Life becomes lifeless. There is loss of adventure and carefreeness.

The Spontaneity Double Bind

As an adult, a male is often accused of not being spontaneous, of being afraid to let go and be playful and uninhibited. He is told he is too self-conscious. When he does let go and express himself in a spontaneous, uninhibited way, he may make those around him uncomfortable.

Either Way He Loses

If he is too serious, he is told to loosen up. If he behaves in a spontaneous, free, and uninhibited way, others may become uncomfortable and accuse him of making a fool out of himself, call him childish, and label his behavior as immature or inappropriate.

A man is always supposed to be ready. Like a baseball player, he is supposed to be in a crouch position, ready to field the ball whenever it comes his way. He can't let down. This results in many men living with generalized anxiety and constant stress in order to meet the demands of work and home. There is no down time. This is part of being a provider. Life becomes one big job. This is why I believe sports are so important to some men—because it is the one arena where a man has permission to "let it all hang out"—be spontaneous—and not be chastised for it.

Have you noticed how alcohol and sports go together in this country? Go to any professional sports venue and you will see grown men having a few beers to "prime the pump" and let it all hang out. Men who have been in control all week now start to let it all out because they know that once the game is over they will have to put the emotions on hold and be in control once again. After the game, they will have to start cranking it out and lose their ability to enjoy the moment and live in the present.

Men who lack spontaneity, I find, also lack intimacy—as if they had an alarm that goes off when they are getting too deeply involved in a relationship. They know that if they get too deeply involved with someone, they might become dependent upon that person, so they keep that person at arm's length. But for a relationship to have intimacy, there must be empathy.

Empathy is the spontaneous ability to understand other people's hurt and be available to help them through that hurt. It is being able to take off my glasses, put on theirs, and see life through their eyes. Empathy is not the same as sympathy. Sympathy is when I see a person drowning and jump in and drown with him or her. Empathy is when I stand at the edge of the pool, see that person's plight, understand the situation, and throw a lifeline. Empathy is being in a position to help.

Many men lack empathy because they have shut down this part in their lives. I have counseled men who seem to be on another planet when their wives express deep emotional pain concerning their relationship. It is not that these men don't care; they have simply been out of touch with this part of themselves for so long that they do not know how to comfort or show compassion.

This lack of spontaneity effects a man's love life as well. As a boy, a male learns that touching, cuddling, stroking—all expressions of physical affection—are for girls. It is not manly to be kissed, hugged, held, and stroked. But when the boy becomes a man, he is expected to be a good lover, and he suddenly learns that this involves the ability to enjoy, freely and comfortably, being touched, cuddled, and stroked—to express physical affection.

Many men, at this point, are caught between a rock and a hard place. A man may feel uncomfortable with affection. As a result his partner may view him as a cold, abrupt, harsh, insensitive, and non-sensual lover. If he tries to be tender, it may seem forced to his partner, and he may not be comfortable with it himself. He may even become sexually inhibited as he strives to be other than he is. This will cause him to question his ability to be the kind of lover that his wife desires. Once again he will be caught in the performance trap because his major goal is to please his wife, but he feels inadequate to do so.

Many couples come to me for counseling because they don't feel they have enough romance in their marriage. The wife desires to be close, which means she wants to cuddle and be held. Often she desires a time of preparation for the event of making love. Women often tell me, "If I have to tell my husband what to do—then it just isn't romantic. It's mechanical!"

But if the husband has been geared to be performance oriented, then he feels he must have the necessary information to be successful. The more information he has the better chance he has to hit the target. A man will often have trouble with cuddling and stroking because this requires him to draw from the softer side of his personality, which he has all but killed and now, all of a sudden, has to bring back to life.

For a woman, making love is an experience; for a man it is an event. A man usually approaches sex as a goal-oriented activity, rather than a playful, sensual interchange and a major source of pleasure and satisfaction. Instead of *making love,* men "have sex."

For men, this area touches upon some deeply seated identity issues. Whether we want to admit it or not, male adequacy is often linked to sexual functioning in the bedroom. If a man has problems in this area, then he often feels he is less than a man. Yet the terms for success are defined by the woman. Once again, he feels caught. Therefore, a man may seek sexual fulfillment from pornography. This is much easier for a man since the woman he fantasizes about is always available and makes no demands. The key question is what keeps a man stuck in the Gender Double Bind when it fosters such devastating results?

JUST WIN, BABY

Al Davis is the owner of the Los Angeles Raiders—the winningest sports franchise in the history of sports. One of Davis's slogans is "Just Win Baby"—a slogan that summarizes the team's philosophy. Losing is a "no-no." Failure is not tolerated. Whatever it takes—win. Men are taught that they must not fail. Listen to Herb Goldberg:

> As a young boy, he is repeatedly given the message that success and winning make him lovable and worthwhile. There is hardly a more devastating label than that of "loser." Some boys get the message in an extreme form through their father's rejection and his intensely negative reaction when they do poorly. Indirectly, the boy gets the message because he is adored when he triumphs. He also observes the powerful positive reaction of his parents to other boys when they are successful winners or prove themselves to be the "best." These early evaluations contaminate his pleasure in many activities as he grows older. If he can't win or do very well at something, he won't do it at all. This progressively narrows his range of involvements until he winds up as primarily a spectator to most activities except those in which he can excel.[4]

The fear of failure can ultimately destroy a man. Like an octopus, it wraps its tentacles around him and holds him day after day. It can prevent him from ever discovering what he really wants because what he doesn't want is much more powerful—he doesn't want to fail. The fear of failure keeps him from experimenting and learning and, most of all, growing. His primary goal is to avoid failure.

Why are so many men afraid to come to counseling with their wives? Simple—fear of being told they have failed. Why do so many men refuse to go to church? Simple, fear of being told how they do not measure up. Even though a man's body and soul may be sending signals to alert him to potential danger—like the red light on the dashboard of a car—he hesitates to heed the signals, check under the hood, and make the necessary repairs, so he ignores the signals and ends up with smoke billowing from under the hood, in need of a major overhaul in his life.

Many men realize early on in life that to become a winner they must compete. If a boy is ever going to amount to anything, he thinks, he must beat the other boys at what they do. A young boy quickly learns whether he is a winner or a loser when it comes time to choose teams for a game. The greatest fear for a boy is to be picked last or made to feel that his team has been "stuck" with him. One of the results of this competitive spirit is that the world becomes merely an arena in which to compete and win, but many men never learn the difference between competing and cooperating. Most men choose to compete.

Think about growing up. I remember when I would walk with a buddy I would say, "Race ya to the corner." Whoever won, we would continue to be friends, but we both knew there would be a time to race again and even the score. If competition becomes a man's major approach to life, it brings with it a distorted view of the world and a false set of assumptions. For instance, in the competitive world, a man's masculinity is based upon such quantifiables as how much money he earns, the size of the office he has, or the position he holds. If a man cannot win, buy, bargain for, or steal it, then it has no value. Even in love men may think in terms of quantity. A wife may say, "You don't say you love me anymore." The husband will snap back, "Didn't I buy you a new dishwasher and get you that new coat? Good grief, what will it take to make you happy?"

How about, "I love you"?

Another assumption of a competitive attitude is that it is always good. A father pushes his son to compete and beat the other boys no matter what the cost. On the playground and in life, some men think, the key thing is to be a good competitor and win. Again, it forces men to define their role in terms of acquiring limited goods as proof of their masculinity and to view every other man as a potential rival for these goods. Do not get me wrong. I think competition can teach us a lot. It can build character. But if we are not careful, we can end up viewing the world in terms of winners and losers—and not much in between.

A man's sweet successes are short lived because each man knows he must keep succeeding—and there is the nagging fear he might possibly fail eventually. The more successes a man has, the less he can afford to fail. The higher up the ladder, the further the fall.

I have observed that the more successful a man becomes, the more driven he is, because to lose what he has gained means failure. If he fails, then he will be looked down upon and lose the status he has gained. It is one thing to reach the top, but it takes a whole lot more energy to stay there. When a man's fear of failure becomes stronger than his desire to grow and develop, then a psychological time bomb starts to tick. The man is caught in the Growth Double Bind.

The Growth Double Bind

The adult male has a need to grow, change, and expand. But he also has a strong need for security and control. To grow, change, and expand takes risks. Taking risks means being vulnerable, but he cannot be vulnerable and in control at the same time.

Either Way He Loses

If he allows himself to grow by changing careers, perhaps, or altering his lifestyle he may face criticism by his peers and family. On the other hand, if he stays put, he feels trapped and stagnant and empty.

Previous successes, no matter how great, do not give a man comfort. They do not count. He must succeed today. I know this is true because I face it myself. There have been times I have thought how sweet it would be to go back to a simpler time when I could just enjoy the simple things of life. I even have joked with my friends that working at a local coffee shop sounded pretty good. I could make cappuccinos and lattes, and the customer would leave satisfied every time. I could leave knowing that the standards are the same every day, predictable and possible. No fear of failure. How does a man conquer this fear? More importantly how does our identity in Christ free us from this bind? Let's look at some good news.

A THEOLOGY OF STRUGGLE

Once there was a little boy who had a cocoon in a bottle. He eagerly waited for it to change into a beautiful butterfly. He was told the worm in the cocoon would go through a process called metamorphosis, after which it would emerge as a butterfly. He could hardly wait. He wanted to see the butterfly emerge with its beautiful multicolored wings. Finally the day arrived. The butterfly began to emerge from the cocoon, struggling to break free. But its wings were stuck. So the little boy decided he would help the butterfly. He took a knife and slit the cocoon open so the butterfly could emerge, but what he saw unnerved him. Instead of beautiful multicolored wings, he saw a butterfly with shriveled wings and a swollen body that could not fly. He could not understand it. He thought he was helping the butterfly out. His dad explained to him that the butterfly needed to struggle because without it, the necessary fluid could not flow into its wings. Through struggle, the butterfly, in essence, exercised its wings and gained the strength it would need to fly.

The same thing happens to you and me. God allows us to struggle, even fail, so that we can be strengthened in our faith—in our "inner" man—so we might be all God intends for us to be. Failure is nothing to be shunned. It is something we must embrace because of how God uses it in our lives.

When was the last time you thanked God for your failures? When was the last time you said, "Lord, if failing is what will produce in me Christlikeness—then bring it on"? Me neither. I have a hard time with failure. But if I really believe Romans 8:28, that "all things work together for good" (KJV), then failure is part of the process. Listen to Romans 5:3–5: "We also rejoice in our sufferings, because we know that suffering produces perseverance; perseverance, character;

and character, hope. And hope does not disappoint us, because God has poured out his love into our hearts by the Holy Spirit, whom he has given us."

Brennan Manning, in his book *The Ragamuffin Gospel,* points out that it is okay to have a "victorious limp." Some days we limp across the finish line. But that is okay because God is not concerned about our winning—he is concerned about our character.

The question I always ask myself when things are not going well is "What is the redemptive value of this experience?" I may not always get the answer immediately, but it will come in time. When a man's identity is in Christ, then there is no such thing as a "fear of failure." Why? Because there is nothing to lose. Success for a believer is whatever makes me look more like Jesus. God accepts us not for what we do, but for whose we are—therefore, we do not fear failure. Brennan Manning puts it this way:

> One morning at prayer, I heard this word: "Little brother, I witnessed a Peter who claimed he did not know me, a James who wanted power in return for service to the Kingdom, a Philip who failed to see the Father in me, and scores of disciples who were convinced I was finished on Calvary. The New Testament has many examples of men and women who started out well and then faltered along the way.
>
> "Yet on Easter night I appeared to Peter. James is not remembered for his ambition but for the sacrifice of his life for me. Philip did see the Father in me when I pointed the way, and the disciples who despaired had enough courage to recognize me when we broke bread at the end of the road to Emmaus. My point, little brother, is this: I expect more failure from you than you expect from yourself."
>
> The man who sees his life as a voyage of discovery and runs the risk of failure has a better feel for faithfulness than the timid man who hides behind the law and never finds out who he is at all.[5]

Winston Churchill put it well when he said, "Success is never final; failure is never fatal. It is courage that counts." You do not need a religion you have to carry—you need a relationship to carry you.

Jesus came to "limp" through life with you at times. The "victorious" Christian life means looking more like Jesus after the trial than before.

There is a golf commercial on TV that features golf professional Hale Irwin, in which he says, "There is no such thing as a bad day for a golfer. There are days in which he plays well and then there are days in which he learns well. But there is no such thing as a bad day for a golfer."

Similarly, there is no such thing as a bad day for a man committed to God. There are days he lives well and then there are days he learns well. But there is no bad day for a man whose identity is in Christ. A man who is not afraid to fail can depend on others when he needs help (the Gender Double Bind) and can be free to live life (the Spontaneity Double Bind) as God intended.

> Do you not know?
> Have you not heard?
> The Lord is the everlasting God,
>   the creator of the ends of the earth.
> He will not grow weary,
>   and his understanding no one can fathom.
> He gives strength to the weary
>   and increases the power of the weak.
> Even youths grow weary,
>   and young men stumble and fall;
>   but those who hope in the Lord
>   will renew their strength.
> They will soar on wings like eagles;
>   they will run and not grow weary,
>   they will walk and not be faint.
> (Isaiah 40:28–31)[6]

DISCUSSION QUESTIONS

1. How competitive do you feel with other men? To feel good about yourself, do you need to be one-up, smarter, more powerful, more accomplished than the men around you?

2. What were the different rules for boys and girls in your family?

3. What was your most recent failure? What did you learn? Did it draw you nearer or push you further from God? If nearer, how? If further away, why?

4. How does your identity in Christ impact your view of failure?

Chapter 4

I Owe, I Owe, So Off to Work I Go

Gordon Dahl, a sociologist, made the following observation: "Most middle-class Americans tend to worship their work, work at their play, and play at their worship. As a result their meanings and values are distorted. Their relationships disintegrate faster than they can keep them in repair and their lifestyle resembles a cast of characters in search of a plot."[1] I find this statement especially true when I replace the phrase "middle-class Americans" with the word "men."

In chapter 2, I pointed out that men tend to get their identity from who they know, what they own, and what they do. While all of these sources relate to a man's performance, "what I do" paves the way for "what I own" and "who I know." More than ever, work—or shall I say overwork?—has become an obsession in our country, especially among men. Workaholism is an addiction that our society not only tolerates but applauds and encourages in both the corporate world and our churches.

Think about it. How do we men define ourselves when someone asks us who we are? We tell them our name, where we live, and then what we *do*! Sam Keen in his book *Fire in the Belly* gives a brilliant insight when he says,

> Preparations for the male ritual of work begin even before the age of schooling. Long before a boy child has a concept of the day after tomorrow, he will be asked by well-meaning but unconscious adults, "What do you want to be when you grow up?" It will not take him long to discover that "I want to be a horse" is not an answer that satisfies most adults. They want to know what men plan to do, what job, profession, occupation we have decided to follow at five years of age! Boys are taught early that they are what they do.[2]

Most married men are called upon to be providers—the primary economic support for their families—and a man is supposed to work regardless of how he feels, whether he enjoys his tasks or not. A generation ago, this single-mindedness built railroads and cities and made this country what it is today. Back then, men did what they did out of economic necessity. Men today still feel this same responsibility, but women are now involved in the work force to a much greater degree. Warren Farrel puts it well when he says,

> Almost every father still retains 24-hour-a-day psychological responsibility for the family's financial well-being. Even women who earn more than their husbands tell me that they know their husbands would support their decision to earn as much or as little as they wish. If a woman marries a successful man, then she knows she will have an option to work or not, but not an obligation. Almost all men see bringing home a healthy salary as an obligation, not an option. A woman today has three options:
>
> > Option 1: Full-time career.
> > Option 2: Full-time family.
> > Option 3: Some combination of career and family.

A man sees himself as having three "slightly different" options:

> Option 1: Work full time.
> Option 2: Work full time
> Option 3: Work full time.

The US bureau of the Census explains that full-time working males work on an average eight hours more per week on their jobs than full-time working females.[3]

Since so many women work today, one would think it would free up the father to be home more with his family, that it would take the pressure off. Yet I find that there is added pressure on the man to work even harder because he is fearful of being dependent, of not being a good provider. Also, a man feels that work is the one last bastion where he at least can have some control in his life. So he works hard to keep it. If a man's identity primarily comes from who he knows, what he owns, and especially from what he *does*, then he must work hard to keep his identity. The one area where a man has power is in the area of economic resources. He may not have power emotionally or relationally, but at least he can show his prowess financially.

But "being a good provider" means more today that it did a generation ago. Today a man not only has to provide for his family economically, but he also has to "be there" emotionally and psychologically for them. A man is now expected to assist in childbirth, change diapers, take part in nightly feedings, take care of the children when they are sick, understand their children's feelings, help with their homework, and the list goes on—all of which is good and healthy. I heartily agree that providing for a family is much more than getting a paycheck, and research has shown that the emotional stability of the family rests not upon the mother, but upon the father.

Still, providing both economically and emotionally requires a tremendous amount of time. This is where I find many men experiencing what is called the Breadwinner Double Bind.

The Breadwinner Double Bind

To be an acceptable husband and father, a man is taught that he must provide his family with the best life possible. He is admired and praised for being a good provider and capable competitor. In the process of striving to make the "good life" a reality, he will be confronted by the complaints of his family that he is not involved enough with them. He is always too tired, works too much, and neglects being husband and father. The compulsive, never-ending demands of an upwardly mobile lifestyle make intimacy increasingly more difficult.

Either Way He Loses

If a man works hard, he may be resented by his family for being neglectful of them and for having misplaced values. If he withdraws from the rat race, however, his family may compare him, as he may compare himself, unfavorably with those who are more successful.

This is exactly how John felt when he came to see me. John, who made good money as a sales representative for a large company, lived with his family in an exclusive neighborhood, his children went to the best schools, and they belonged to the local country club, where his wife played tennis. But John said his family complained of his lack of involvement with them due to his extensive travel schedule. So he took some time off and cut back on his travel in order to stay home. As a result, his sales dropped somewhat, and his family was forced to forego some of the amenities to which they had grown accustomed. They could no longer afford the country club membership, and some of the children's expensive extracurricular school activities might possibly have to be cut.

Now, said John, his family was complaining that they really needed to stay in the country club because all of the children's friends belonged and the children would be heartbroken if they could not go on some of the trips planned by the school. So John began to increase his work load to meet these so-called needs.

"Rod," he told me, "I just can't win. Not only that, but when I'm at home, my wife and kids are so used to operating without me that I end up having huge fights with them because I wasn't there when many of their decisions were made. I feel like my role is just to 'feed the machine.'"

John was caught in the Breadwinner Double Bind. John's case also suggests another bind that flows out of a man's heavy involvement at work: the Child-Rearing Double Bind.

The Child-Rearing Double Bind

When a working father takes an active part in rearing children, he and his wife may clash over child-rearing philosophy and attitudes implemented while he was at work. He may feel resented for interfering, messing up the system, and creating problems. If, on the other hand, he tries to stay out of the picture by allowing his wife to be the principal authority, or if he is too lenient and fails to back up his wife when she tries to discipline the children, then he may be resented for being a passive or uninvolved father, or he may be accused of trying to be the "good guy" while Mom has to be the "bad guy." He may then slowly withdraw, and his influence in the family—and the depth of his relationship with his children—will steadily diminish.

Either Way He Loses

If he tries to involve himself heavily in child-rearing, he may be resented for being a divisive influence. If he tries to stay out of the picture, he may be resented for being passive and uninvolved.

Ultimately, a man caught in the Child-Rearing Double Bind will find work to be a refuge from home because at least there he can have some control over his world. This type of withdrawal greatly affects children. It affects his daughter because she does not see in her father a solid, involved picture of masculinity. It has been said that the first man a girl falls in love with is her father. If he withdraws, then she will get her ideas about relationships with the opposite sex from another source, namely, television. Could this be why soap operas and romance novels (which I call "fantasy pornography") are so popular? People often resort to fantasy when they lack fulfillment in reality.

The biggest loser when a dad abdicates involvement, however, is the son. It takes a man to grow a man. If the son does not have a template to pattern himself after, then where does he go for his identity? Listen to Ted Dobson: "Brokenness in men is due to the fact that boys lack sufficient contact with their fathers to generate a healthy masculine self-image. Indeed, the macho characteristic of appearing remote simply reflects the remoteness of fathers from their sons. If the father defines masculinity for the boy and is physically or emotionally distant from his son, then he communicates that manliness is a matter of standing aloof from others."[4]

A father who is absent during the day and returns at 6:00 P.M. usually gives his children his temper, not his teaching. The family, and especially sons, lose the presence of the father and thus *the* role model of what it means to be a man.

Why do some men stay on the work treadmill? Let me give you a few reasons.

YOU NEED THIS CAR

A Nissan car commercial once insisted, "You need this car." The commentator then listed the virtues of owning the car and how it would make life easier. The ad sounded as though the owner of such a car would automatically be happy and reach a new level of satisfaction by just buying the car.

Clearly, society teaches that it is not okay to be content. Reaching the next level of prestige or success is always the goal. If one can just reach the next level, whatever that may be, *then* happiness and joy will be achieved. Many men buy into the notion that external success is the manly road to contentment and security. A man must do whatever is required to hone a competitive edge in order to gain status, power, and wealth, and reach the next level.

Most men expend far more energy than is required for their family's happiness. I will never forget one man who came to see me for counseling. I will call him Mike. He was making only about $20,000 a year; he and his wife had five children ranging in age from one to ten. Mike was obsessed with getting a Rolex watch someday. In spite of his family's financial needs, he would constantly squirrel away money to buy the watch. Finally, he got a deal; he found one for $5000. He proudly wore the watch and showed it off even though everyone knew he couldn't afford it. But just the illusion of reaching the next level gave Mike a sense of pride and status. He had a Rolex. He eventually lost his wife and family in the process.

FANTASYLAND

Another reason a man relentlessly pursues his work is to fulfill his wife's desires and his own dreams. It is my belief that men and women enter marriage with a certain "idea" or "fantasy" of what marriage should offer. I believe the primary fantasy of many women is for a husband who will provide security so that she can devote her energy to work, home, children, or a combination of those. Women in this generation, consciously or unconsciously, expect their husbands to provide material things as tokens of their love. The church has helped support this notion: the wife is supposed to be a supportive helpmate, while the husband is supposed to provide financially. This fantasy of marriage often leads a woman to derive her significance from her husband's, so that both the husband's *and* the wife's significance is relative to the man's success. But the typical woman also has a second fantasy that is just as powerful. She also wants passion, respect, excitement, and gentleness from this one man.

A man's fantasy is often that since he has now "settled" on this one woman and taken himself out of the "dating game," this one woman is now obligated to take care of his every emotional and physical need. She is to be constantly available when he needs the emotional support and physical expression of intimacy—that is, sex.

What often happens in marriage is that both partners become disappointed—even fearful—in their relationship. A wife may fear that if she expresses her dissatisfaction in her husband's lack of passion or gentility or whatever, she may lose her security. So she "stuffs" her feelings and doesn't rock the boat. At this point she may turn to romance novels or soap operas or even an extramarital affair.

The man, on the other hand, may become so consumed by providing for his wife's primary fantasy (financial security) that he ends up being too tired to be romantic. He also recognizes, as the old saying goes: "If Momma ain't happy, ain't nobody happy." The wife usually becomes the emotional franchise in a man's life. It's a fact that in a divorce, a man experiences ten times the emotional suffering that a woman does. The wife often has a greater emotional support network, but the husband has consumed himself in work and has neglected that part of himself. The primary validator for a man is a woman, and if she is no longer present then there goes his emotional support. Men realize that the primary validators of our masculinity are women. We know but hate to admit to the fact that we are especially dependent on women to nurture and affirm us as men.

As a marriage counselor, I have seen men bite their lips and walk away from arguments with their wives. Why? Because they do not want to risk the tremendous loss that might result if they engaged their wives in an argument. Yet the wife interprets his walking away as his opinion that the relationship is not worth fighting for. Men work so hard to fulfill the first fantasy of their wives (financial security) that they forget about the second (intimacy).

MOVIN' ON UP

I used to watch the television comedy *The Jeffersons*. George Jefferson was a successful black man in the dry-cleaning business who had done so well that he was able to buy a condominium in the elite downtown section, for, as the show's theme song stated, he was "Movin' on up." But movin' on up also meant leaving something behind. George often lacked the tact and sophistication necessary to cope with his new surroundings. To compensate, he would buy "things" to demonstrate his prowess and justify his presence in the upper echelons of society. George would probably have felt more comfortable if he had stayed in his old neighborhood, but he had to move up because that is what a man is supposed to do. George got caught in a bind that many men experience today: the Career-Ladder Double Bind.

The Career-Ladder Double Bind

To be a success, a man thinks he must be upwardly mobile, strive for promotions, and take on greater responsibilities. In the process, however, he often gives up those things he does best, that originally attracted him to his work and gave him deep satisfaction. As he advances, he finds it increasingly difficult to relate to his former friends and coworkers. But if he contents himself with staying where he is—that is, if he doesn't move up the ladder—then he may be viewed as unsuccessful and become vulnerable to those who pass him by. They will then be "movin' on up" and leaving him behind.

Either Way He Loses

If he maintains upward vocational mobility in the pursuit of success, he may lose the inner joy and satisfaction of doing what he once did best. He may also lose close friends who can no longer relate to him comfortably. If he allows himself to stay where he is, he may look around and see others passing him by. This could result in his accusing himself of being a failure, lacking ambition, and failing to give the best to his family.

Many men are caught in the Career-Ladder Double Bind because they think the only way they have to fulfill their dreams is through the vehicle of work. In our society of specialization, if a man wants to get ahead he has to think about how to gain a competitive edge, which in turn means moving up the ladder so that he can have the resources necessary to achieve his goals.

It seems there are no more Renaissance men. A Renaissance man is one who has several areas in his life that give him pleasure. He is not defined by one activity. The Renaissance men of old were not only master craftsmen but men who loved music, literature, and a variety of other areas that filled out their lives. That was then. Now, because of such a driven society we cannot afford to take the time to develop other areas in our lives. We live in a driven society. Robert Hemfelt, Frank Minirth, and Paul Meier put it this way:

> Every day we are bombarded with slogans that warn us that we only go around once, that we should reach for the gusto, and that we ought to be all that we can be. Any way we turn we encounter more information to absorb, new skills to learn, more tasks to complete. We encounter information overload every time we snap on the television or listen to the radio. An average week-day edition of the *New York Times* now contains more data than a person in the seventeenth century was likely to encounter in a life-time! Somehow we have to consume this volume of information if we want to stay ahead of the pack.[5]

We no longer have time limits in our culture. We can order from catalogues twenty-four hours a day, get money from the ATM machine at any time, and even send a FAX from the car. An electronics firm in New York has produced a watch that can keep track of your daily schedule. It will play soft, soothing music to remind you of your next appointment, but if you ignore the music it will replace it with a harsh message: "Please, hurry. Please, hurry. Please, hurry!" I want one of those for Christmas! Don't you? . . . Right!

The problem with this single vehicle of work to achieve our dreams is the unpredictability of the workplace. Our specialty may be in demand one day but on the rocks the next. A man's goals may really be in the hands of others. It takes the cooperation of others, namely his workplace, to help him get where he desires to go.

So what happens if a man gets laid off? He becomes angry and faces the realization that he has to start over if he is to fulfill his dreams. Then every decision becomes pivotal, because the later in life he has to begin again, the more pressure he feels to catch up to reach his goals. Time is running out. At this point a man can go one of two ways. He can become angry and explosive or he can become passive and just give up.

FATIGUE IS NEXT TO GODLINESS

There seems to be a belief among Christians, men especially, that the more exhausted we are, the more committed we must be, and, thereby, the more we can gain God's approval. Even though we pay lip service to the concept of grace, most of us really believe we are supposed to get our salvation the old fashioned way—by earning it. I am convinced that the enemy has convinced us that unless we are worn to a frazzle, running here and there, we cannot possibly be a dedicated Christian.

To justify overwork, we baptize it in the Puritan work ethic, which is different than the Protestant work ethic. The Protestant work ethic goes back to Martin Luther. Luther strongly reacted to the Catholic priests who believed they were the only ones who had access to God and that their calling was more valuable than anyone else's. Luther wanted to make it clear that every man has access to God and the Scriptures, and that every man's calling, whether milking cows or making shoes, was just as valuable to God as the priests'. Luther made it clear that whenever a man used his gifts, God would get the glory. That is the Protestant work ethic.

This idea of work ties into the last reason men have a tendency to stay on the work treadmill.

TELL ME I COUNT

Samuel Osherson, in his book *Finding Our Fathers,* studied business executives who had graduated from Harvard more than twenty years earlier. As he interviewed these men, Dr. Osherson discovered that even though they were successful executives, they still had unfinished business with their fathers.

> There are numerous circumstances in adult life that leave us feeling childlike—needy, helpless, powerless to change things. In growing up men have great difficulty coming to terms with dependency and vulnerability, often because our fathers showed us that such feelings were unacceptable, that to be successful men, to win our fathers' approval, achievement was what counted. Our vulnerability and dependency became papered over by an instrumental, competent pose as adults or by focusing on what we do well: our ability to achieve in the work world.[6]

Every man, as I have already pointed out, wants one thing from his father—his blessing. If he does not get the blessing from his dad, he will work hard to prove he is worthy of it.

Take Bob. At forty-two, he was on the verge of losing everything—his home, his wife, his children, his health—everything. He told me that he was tired of trying to prove himself to his father and that maybe his dad was right after all. I said, "What do you mean?"

Bob said about ten years ago his father was lying in the hospital on his deathbed. He had never heard his dad say, "I love you" or "I believe in you." In fact, he had heard the opposite. He said his father called him over to his bedside. Bob went over and leaned down so his father could whisper in his ear what he was going to say. Bob thought this might be it, he might finally hear "I love you" from his dad. His dad said, "Son, the business is now in your hands. I hope you can handle it, but I doubt it. You will probably mess this up just like everything else." His father died a few hours later.

Bob set out to prove his dad wrong. He heard his voice every day. He burned out because he never knew when enough was enough. Every man longs to know he counts. Every man longs to know that he makes a difference. Even Jesus needed to hear from his Father, "This is my beloved son in whom I am well pleased" before he did anything. A man will stay on the treadmill because he has something to prove—that he counts.

GETTING OFF THE TREADMILL

So how does one get off of the treadmill of work? How do we break this bind? Are we stuck with what Henry David Thoreau once wrote: "The laboring man has not leisure for a true integrity day by day. He has no time to be anything but a machine."

I want to make something very clear. I am not against work. Work is a good thing. It helps us to reflect the image of God within us. One of the purposes God has given to us as his special creation is to have responsible dominion (Gen. 2:15–16 and Gen. 1:28). Work is an expression of rulership. It is therefore good for us to pursue our work with diligence, honesty, and pride. But God has called us not to be frantic but to be faithful. Work today has become the biggest single factor in defining who we are—our identity as men.

What do we need to do to break out of the bind of overwork? What is it going to take for us to get our identity back? This is a delicate issue because it may involve a change in lifestyle. We are so imbued with a strong work ethic that it is hard for us to imagine that we could be valued apart from our performance as men.

Let me ask you a question. Do you believe that a person is valuable totally apart from what he or she can produce? This is the place we must begin if we are going to break out of the Breadwinner Double Bind.

The way to begin to break out of the Breadwinner Double Bind is to recognize that our identity comes from "whose we are" not from what we do. As a man, I must come to grips with the fact I do not live to work—but I work to live and that even work becomes vanity if it is devoid of the blessing of God (Eccl. 3:13). So what must I realize in order to keep my work in perspective and draw my identity from Christ? Let me give you some suggestions.

1. Recognize That "I Am What I Earn" Is a Myth

Studies indicate that the wealthiest men in society are often the angriest. It seems that when a man does not have enough, he is angry because he cannot buy all of the toys he wants. But when he has more than he needs, he is still angry because the toys he can now buy do not fulfill him so he always seeks another level to get a bigger toy to find an even bigger disappointment.

Jesus made it clear when he said, "If anyone would come after me, he must deny himself and take up his cross and follow me. For whoever wants to save his life will lose it, but whoever loses his life for me and for the gospel will save it. What good is it for a man to gain the whole world, yet forfeit his soul? Or what can a man give in exchange for his soul?" (Mark 8:34–36).

Our work will not last for eternity—but our relationship with God will. A man must start with an attitude of contentment. The moment I stop comparing my financial scorecard with others and am thankful for what God has given me; that is the moment I begin to feel better about myself. The apostle Paul said, "I have learned to be content whatever the circumstances. I know what it is to be in need, and I know what it is to have plenty. I have learned the secret of being content in any and every situation, whether well fed or hungry, whether living in plenty or in want" (Phil. 4:11–12). A man who opts to be satisfied with what he has will have more time and energy for the kinds of nurturing relationships that will meet his basic needs. If I am able to be content with what I have, then whatever is extra is gravy.

2. Live in the Here and Now

Most of our lack of contentment comes from focusing on the future or fretting over the past. Often we are like the children of Israel in the wilderness. God promised to give them manna every day, and he told them to collect only what they needed for that day. But some tried to collect enough for the next day as well. They found out the next day that the manna they had gathered turned into worms and was useless. Similarly, God gives us enough grace for today. We may try to stretch that grace into the next day, but sure enough, it turns into worms. We must enjoy the daily grace God gives us.

Jesus put it well when he said,

> See how the lilies of the of the field grow. They do not labor
> or spin. Yet I tell you that not even Solomon in all his splendor

was dressed like one of these. If that is how God clothes the grass of the field, which is here today and tomorrow is thrown into the fire, will he not much more clothe you, O you of little faith? So do not worry, saying, "What shall we eat?" or "What shall we wear?" For the pagans run after all these things, and your heavenly Father knows that you need them. But seek first his kingdom and his righteousness, and all these things will be given to you as well. Therefore do not worry about tomorrow, for tomorrow will worry about itself. Each day has enough trouble of its own. (Matthew 6:28–34)

3. Take Time Out

Jesus had a fixed perspective—an eternal perspective. But how did he maintain it? He was obedient, especially in the area of resting—taking time out. Did you know that it is a command to rest? Read Genesis 2:1–3. On the seventh day, God did not rest because he was exhausted or couldn't think of anything else to do. But he stopped anyway. He made it a priority. Jesus, in Mark 6:30–32 purposely sought relief from the crowds to get some rest. And Jesus accomplished everything his Father had sent him to do. Rest is not a suggestion from God; it's a command.

4. Recognize That God Has Called You to Be a Good Husbandman

A husbandman is a farming term for one who "takes care of the farm." Growing up on a farm, I quickly realized that if I paid too much attention to one field or one group of animals all of the other fields and animals would go neglected. I constantly had to be checking all of the fields and all of the animals to make sure that I was producing an environment where their optimal growth could occur.

It is not by coincidence that God called Adam to be, in effect, the "husbandman" of the garden. It was Adam's job to be a good steward and provide an atmosphere for the growth of its inhabitants, namely the animals, plant life, and his family.

Similarly, God has called you and I as men to be good husband-men of our gardens, namely our children and our wives. It is our job to create an environment free of weeds and impediments to their growth. This requires us to take the time to find out what their needs are and to provide for them in those areas. I have found that if we concentrate too much in one area, namely financial provision, then the weeds will sprout in the other areas, namely our relationship with God, wife, and children.

A good husbandman sees life holistically and realizes that God will call him to account. By the way, being a good husbandman also means that God has called me to be a good steward of—*me*! I believe that God is going to ask us when we appear before the judgment how we took care of ourselves physically, mentally, socially, intellectually, and spiritually. You are as much a gift of God as your friends and family. Take care of it.

I agree with the friar from a Nebraska monastery who wrote this poem later in life.

> If I had my life to live over again, I'd try to make more mistakes next time, would relax, I would limber up, I would be sillier than I have been this trip.
> I know of very few things I would take seriously. I would take more trips.
> I would be crazier.
> I would climb more mountains, swim more rivers, and watch more sunsets.
> I would do more walking and looking.
> I would eat more ice cream and less beans.
> I would have more actual troubles and fewer imaginary ones.
> You see, I'm one of those people who live life prophylactically and sensibly hour after hour, day after day.
> Oh, I've had my moments, and if I had to do it over again I'd have more of them.
> In fact, I'd try to have nothing else, just moments, one after another, instead of living so many years ahead each day.

I've been one of those people who never go anywhere without a ther-
    mometer, a hot-water bottle, a gargle, a raincoat, aspirin, and a
    parachute.
If I had to do it over again I would go places, do things, and travel
    lighter than I have.
If I had my life to live over I would start barefooted earlier in the
    spring and stay that way later in the fall.
I would play hooky more.
I wouldn't make such good grades, except by accident.
I would ride on more merry-go-rounds.
I'd pick more daisies.[7]

Amen!!

DISCUSSION QUESTIONS

1. How do you react to Gordon Dahl's statement, "Americans
   tend to worship their work, work at their play, and play at
   their worship"? Why?
2. What are the factors in your personal and work life that cause
   the most stress?
3. How much is enough? How would you know?
4. Define *husbandman*. On a scale of 1 to 10, where are you in
   this area? What have you done well and what do you need to
   improve?
5. How does identity in Christ effect your view of work and
   worth?

CHAPTER 5

No Fear

He was cool, calm, and collected whenever there was trouble. No matter what he did or where he went, danger and excitement were sure to follow. His name was Dirty Harry—played by Clint Eastwood in the movies. I remember one scene in particular. Harry had just gone into a diner to get a cup of coffee and something to eat. No big deal, just a simple meal. But not when Harry was around. Apparently there was a bank robbery taking place next door and one of the robbers comes into the restaurant where Harry was eating. The robber grabs one of the customers and tells everyone not to move. Harry, as I remember, quickly throws hot coffee on the robber, grabs his gun, and then shoots the guy with it. He then leaves the diner to take on the other robbers. He is deadly accurate with his Magnum 45 and shoots one of the robbers in the arm. Harry walks toward the robber whose gun is only a few inches from his other hand. Harry sees the gun laying near the robber, and with his own Magnum 45 still drawn, he says his now-classic line, "Go ahead, make my day." The robber slowly pulls his hand back and Harry apprehends him.

We not only have Dirty Harry (Clint Eastwood) today but we also have the blue-collar macho man Rambo (played by Sylvester

Stallone), the all-out risk-taker John McClain (Bruce Willis) in the *Die Hard* movies, and of course the Terminator (Arnold Schwarzenegger), and Robocop. What do all of these characters of the screen have in common? They are heroes. They take control, they punish their enemies, and they come out of the most deadly situations unscathed. They dare to do the unimaginable and take the greatest risks because that is what a man is supposed to do.

I find that many men have this same mentality when it comes to living everyday life. I call it the Hero Image Double Bind.

The Hero Image Double Bind

As a boy grows up, he will be indoctrinated with what it means to be a hero. To be a hero, one must take hazardous risks and accept challenges to masculinity even when doing so may be harmful. Behaving courageously often means denying fear (living in denial) and plunging into dangerous situations to prove oneself. For example, if a boy is challenged by another boy to a fight—even if one of the boys knows he is outmatched and will get the tar beat out of him—and he doesn't accept the challenge, he will be accused of being a wimp—in other words, unmanly.

Either Way He Loses

If he accepts the challenge, assumes the risk, confronts dangers head on, he is likely to get in over his head and end up really hurting himself physically or emotionally. If he backs away from the challenge or wants to give it some thought, then he might be seen as unmanly by his peers. This is a no-win situation.

A certain mystique comes with being the hero—the guy who always comes through in a clutch. This myth appeals to many men who have little control in their lives and seem powerless to do anything about it. But there is a heavy price to pay for being a hero: alienation, isolation, physical injury, possible mental illness produced by stress, and a possible early death. Aaron Kipnis has helped me gain the following insights about the Hero Image Double Bind.[1] It usually leads to:

1. *Workaholism.* We talked about this in the last chapter, but suffice it to say a man will overwork in order to bury his fears, cover up his emptiness, and avoid his anxieties about having intimate relationships. Workaholism then leads to:

2. *Loss of emotions.* A man will no longer feel. He will "numb out." Often when a man comes home from work, he wants to be left alone. He "gave at the office" and is often too tired to interact. When he does interact, everyone walks on eggshells for fear he may explode. He may be a dynamo at work, but he is a zombie at home. He may be experiencing what I call the Feeling Double Bind.

The Feeling Double Bind

Throughout his life, if a man expresses his feelings openly and really cries, screams, and lets it all hang out, he may be seen as unstable or neurotic. If he controls his feelings carefully, he will inevitably become guarded, hidden, and emotionally unknown to himself and others—even angry.

Either Way He Loses

If he lets it all hang out, he is considered immature, lacking in self-control. If he contains his emotions, he is considered secretive, distant, and overly self-controlled.

Boys learn early that girls are permitted to have feelings, but if a boy expresses his feelings, it often makes his peers, parents, and other adults uneasy. In other words, feelings are not masculine. Boys are constantly being told that they must not whine, complain, or cry when they are hurt. When these boys grow up they have learned an important lesson—men should suffer alone and in silence. So what does it take for a man to feel again?

3. *An addiction to excitement.* To counter the numbness, a man may adopt habits that provide stimulation and intensity. He may get involved in addictions such as alcohol, drugs, pornography, or sex. He may find himself starting fights with his wife just to stir things. The numbness, finally, leads to:

4. *Loss of soul.* A man will often feel disconnected and empty. He will look inside and not find much of anything to hold on to. I compare this condition to a light bulb I replaced the other day. It did not have that gray burned-out look to it. It was clear and looked like everything was in tact. But upon further examination I found that the wires inside the light bulb were split and could not carry the electricity to light up the bulb. Many men are like that light bulb. Everything looks okay on the outside but the wires are cut on the inside—they feel disconnected. But how did we get this way?

HEROES ARE MADE—NOT BORN

In his book *Touching: The Human Significance of the Skin,* Ashley Montague quotes a number of studies that show how infant boys in America receive fewer demonstrative acts of affection from their mothers than infant girls. They are touched less. The author concludes that this may be one of the reasons men are more reticent about touching than women. Other studies indicate that infant boys are more likely to be held outward, toward the world and other people, while little girls were held inward, toward the security, warmth, and comfort of the parents. Girl toddlers are much more likely to get help and comfort when they cry or hurt themselves than boy toddlers. When a boy gets hurt, he is often told to keep his cool: "take it like a man," "hold your mud," "keep a stiff upper lip," "grin and bear it," "suck it up."

I will never forget one incident. I once saw a little boy walking through the airport, and not looking where he was going, he ran into a chair that was bolted to the ground. I heard the crack of his knee when it hit the steel legs of the chair. I—as an adult—would have cried if I had run into it, and so did this boy. His father, seeing this unmanly display of emotion, calmly walked over to his son and said, "Dry it up—dry it up right now." I interpreted this as male talk for "quit crying; you're acting like a girl and embarrassing me." The boy did all that he could not to cry and limped onto the plane with his dad.

That little boy learned that a part of being a man was how he dealt with his pain. A man's pain is not to be shown outwardly. Instead a man is to just swallow his pain and anger. Therefore, men learn to deal with their pain and anger covertly.

This attitude of "taking the pain"—or "no pain, no gain"—is reinforced through the games we play.

PLAYING HURT

I remember watching the NFL title game between the San Francisco 49ers and the Dallas Cowboys. This was billed as being the "real" Superbowl, for whoever won this game was virtually assured of winning the Superbowl. What made the game so intriguing, however, was the fact that the star running back for the Dallas Cowboys was hurt. He had a tender hamstring, and it was announced that he might not play. Emmit Smith was vital to the success of the Cowboys. In essence, if he did not play, they probably would not win. Everybody was watching when the Cowboys' offense came out onto the field. Sure enough, there was Emmit, ready to play through the pain. He played incredibly well, and he showed no signs of his injury. Yet as each quarter went on, you could see him begin to limp slightly. He was like a tire with a slow leak. Each quarter a little more air leaked out until, in the fourth quarter, Emmit went flat. One good tackle in the fourth quarter put Emmit out of commission, but not without loud applause from the crowd who had watched him give his 110 percent while playing hurt. That is what heroes are supposed to do.

We cheer the sports hero who, after being smashed to smithereens on the playing field, gets up and plays hurt. But what about those who do not recover and are hurt for life? How many old football players do you know? Yeah, me neither. Many athletes with injured legs can only play because their trainers simply wrap their injury tighter and give them drugs to numb the pain. The number of players in professional sports who resort to drugs like alcohol, cocaine, and painkillers is astonishing.

What happens on the playing field translates quite well into life. Every man today, in some way or another, plays hurt and often has something to numb the pain. Yet we also learn that "to the hero goes the spoils." Football, hockey, and other contact sports emphasize to a young man that enduring pain and forgoing pleasure ensures him of winning intimacy and success. In other words, the hero gets the girl. The affection of women and admiration of older men usually comes from being the hero. Who gets the cheerleaders' attention? The hero.

Young women also are caught in a bind. They may not be forced into athletic competition with each other, but they are conditioned that they should not give love, attention, and intimacy to a man who does not demonstrate heroic qualities. Please do not misunderstand me. I am not against contact sports. There are a lot of good qualities that can come from being in team sports. But all too often it is the superstar who gets rewarded—the one who can perform—and not the team. When sports are done right, a man can learn that he needs to have a team around him to succeed; he can learn that to cooperate and compromise do not mean failure. He can learn from sports to think strategically and gain physical discipline. He can learn mastery of a skill. These traits can be very helpful to a man in leading a more balanced and healthy life. Without these traits he might learn merely a "survival of the fittest" mentality.

And what about the guy who doesn't play and has other interests? He also does not fare well. How many men do you know would be excited if their son came home and said, "Dad, I want to be an interior decorator" (or nurse, artist, or math whiz)? Often these boys get labeled as nerds, wimps, sissies, losers, creeps, or are seen as too sensitive—and not just among the other guys. Even the girls sometimes see certain pursuits as less heroic. Often these young men grow up with a sense of anger just beneath the surface—like a volcano—until something happens that is either destructive or puts them in a mental ward. Research shows that young boys are admitted to mental hospitals and juvenile institutions about seven times more frequently than girls of similar age and socioeconomic background. It is easy to see how boys sometimes grow into control-oriented and insensitive men.

There is also another possible factor that contributes to the Hero Image Double Bind.

YOU'RE IN THE ARMY NOW

I had the opportunity to be the master of ceremonies for a Promise Keepers Conference in Houston, Texas, with 42,569 men in attendance. One of the speakers, Stu Weber, is from a military background and exudes confidence and conviction, though he also shows tenderness and compassion as well. I will never forget what happened during his message. He talked about sacrifice and commitment, and then he asked the men present who had fought in the unpopular Vietnam War to stand. Several thousand stood. Then Stu said, "Gentlemen, let's give these men the welcome home today that they did not get when they first came home." More than forty thousand men stood as one and cheered with wild applause. The vets began to hug each other and cry loudly as they finally were given permission to grieve their woundedness and be accepted again as sons of America. They finally received a hero's welcome. They were finally told "thank you" for what they had done and that what they did counted. These men were finally given a sense of purpose for their pain.

The United States military is second only to athletics in being portrayed as a social entity that makes real men out of boys. In their posters the Marines tout that if you join them you will become a man. Yet, as with sports, such masculinity is often judged solely on physical prowess.

There is no question that God has called men to be protectors— to be warriors. It is a biblical mandate. Stu Weber puts it well when he says,

> The heart of a Warrior is a protective heart. The Warrior shields, defends, stands between, and guards. According to Moore and Gillette, he invests himself in "the energy of self-disciplined, aggressive action." By warrior I do not mean one who loves war or

draws sadistic pleasure from fighting or bloodshed. There is a difference between a warrior and a brute. A Warrior is a protector. Whether he is stepping on intruding bugs or checking out the sounds that go bump in the night. Whether he is confronting a habitually abusive little league coach or shining a flashlight into a spooky basement. Whether he is shoveling snow or helping women and children into the last lifeboat on the Titanic. Men stand tallest when they are protecting and defending.

A Warrior is one who possesses high moral standards, and holds to high principles. He is willing to live by them, stand for them, spend himself in them, and if necessary die for them. No warrior ever made that more obvious than Jesus of Nazareth. He who is the ultimate Peacemaker will establish that peace from the back of a great white horse as the head of the armies of heaven.[2]

The Scripture shows that Jesus did not always choose to fight if it did not fit his overall purpose. There were times he backed away. In John's gospel, chapter 5, we see Jesus slipping away through the crowd so as not to be stoned. Another time, when Jesus was taken to be thrown off a cliff by an unruly mob, he threw them all back to protect himself but did not "vanquish" them. There was also the time Jesus proclaimed he could call forth a legion of angels but chose not to because it did not fulfill his purpose for being here on earth. A warrior knows when to fight and when to walk away because he lives by a higher principle and purpose.

Protection is different than aggression. Aggression means I must win at any cost. Protection says I have certain values and will do whatever it takes to keep and defend them. Aggression is offensive. Protection is defensive. The biblical warrior always lives his life for a higher purpose and calling, namely to glorify God through his life. Every battle is fought with a strategy that is beyond the present and has a higher purpose in mind. Stu Weber told me that the day before General Norman Schwarzkopf went into battle in Desert Storm, he wrote letters to his children. In these letters he told them how much he loved them and missed them. Stu also told me that Schwarzkopf made it clear to his children that they meant more to him than anything on earth and *that* was why he was fighting in Desert Storm. Not because he loved war, not to be a hero, but because he loved and wanted to protect them. Norman Schwarzkopf is a biblical warrior—he fought with a higher purpose and calling in mind.

In the military a man is trained to repress the pain so he can function effectively and follow orders. If he is not careful he can slowly desensitize himself and lose sight of his purpose. He also can feel that he is disposable—simply "cannon fodder." One key difference between men and women is that men have always been expected to resort to violence when necessary. In fact, a man can begin to operate from the irrational axiom, "I conquer, therefore I am." If this conquest mentality becomes a man's major way of thinking then winning becomes the goal. Also, since I am disposable, let me grab for all of the gusto I can because I may not be here tomorrow to enjoy it. If a man does not have a higher calling to his "warriorhood," he can find himself becoming a mercenary or self-centered and resort to a win-at-all-costs philosophy. As Stu Weber would say, he would become "a brute."

Here are some characteristics of such a mercenary man.

1. *He identifies action with aggression and force.* He has to be in control and will be abusive and use force if necessary to maintain his control.

2. *He has a competitive worldview.* Everything he does is a contest. Relationships, work, and sports are ways to prove his superiority. There is no sense of teamwork. Today we have "free agency" in sports. The highest bidder gets the athlete's loyalty—or if he does not like what he has, he will break the contract to get a better one. I remember one father who played a game of racquetball with his less-experienced teenage son. He would let the boy get close to winning then he would pull out all of the stops to beat his son by the necessary points. I asked him why he did not allow his son to have a taste of victory. He said, "Are you kidding? He might as well learn now that you have to *earn* winning. Besides, *I* like to win."

3. *He exhibits all-or-none thinking.* There is a tendency to oversimplify complex issues and screen out any information that would keep him from winning. There is an attitude that you are either for me or against me.

4. *He represses fear, compassion, and guilt.* The motto "No Fear" that is displayed on various articles of clothing is this man's motto. He does not allow emotions to get in the way. The rules are more important than any relationship.

5. *He dishonors women.* A soldier without a calling would say to a woman, "Since I am laying my life on the line for you, you owe me." There is a sense in which the woman becomes an object to service his needs rather than a person with whom he is to have a relationship.

The military can be effective in helping boys become men, but only *if* it helps keep their purpose and passion intact.

CRASH AND BURN

One of the major results of buying into the Hero Image Double Bind is that a man also gets caught in the Health Double Bind.

The Health Double Bind

As a boy, a male is taught that it is unmasculine to complain about physical pains and illness. "Real men" do not give in to injuries (remember Emmit Smith?) unless the symptoms are severe (like death). Being concerned with health and the body is considered weak, self-indulgent, or hypochondriac behavior. At the same time he is bombarded about the importance of maintaining good health and physical fitness.

Either Way He Loses

If a man is sensitive to his body's distress signals—by taking good care of himself, going to bed when fatigued or not feeling well, and refusing to work under those conditions—his masculinity is questioned. But if he ignores his body's signals and takes it "like a man"—rising above his injuries and pushing himself until he is forced to stop—he will be considered brave, but he may be laying the foundations for chronic illness and possibly early death.

Could this possibly be why men on the average live seven to ten years less than women?

One friend of mine, Richard, was caught in this bind. He and his wife were taking a walk down their driveway to get the mail. About halfway down the driveway Richard collapsed. His wife ran and called 911. After arriving at the hospital and stabilizing Richard, the doctors told him he had a mild heart attack. They asked him if he had been feeling anything unusual in his chest. He said, "Well, for about six months I have been feeling some tightness in my chest but hey, you learn just to live with those things." *Six months!!!* They said it was a wonder he did not have a massive heart attack and die. Heroes are not allowed to get sick. Remember—they play hurt.

The most dangerous professions are traditionally filled by men. They are also much more likely to be injured on the job than women. Could it be that these accidents are due in part to men not being as alert as they could be if they had taken better care of themselves? Author Warren Farrel in his book, *The Myth of Male Power,* gives these statistics:

1. Ninety-four percent of occupational deaths occur to men.
2. The United States has a worker death rate three to four times higher than Japan's. If the U.S. had the same rate we would save the lives of approximately 6000 men and 400 women each year.
3. The United States has only one job safety inspector for every six fish and game inspectors.
4. Every hour of every work day, one construction worker in the United States loses his life.
5. The more hazardous the job, the greater the percentage of men. For example:
   Fire fighting: 99 percent male
   Logging: 98 percent male
   Trucking (heavy): 98 percent male
   Construction: 98 percent male
   Coal Mining: 97 percent male[3]

Heroes do the jobs that are most dangerous, but they also cannot afford to have an off day. If they do, it may cost them dearly both physically and emotionally. But the most important question is—how do we break the Hero Image Double Bind and all that goes with it? Where do we start? Let's take a look.

A MAN'S MAN COUNTS THE COST

A man who always has to win and can never be wrong suffers from a tremendous need for approval, and his identity comes from winning and telling the stories of the conquests and victories of his life. Failure or walking away is not an option.

But a man who is secure in his identity in Christ recognizes he has all the approval he will ever need. Like cosmic Cinderellas, we were rescued by our Prince, the Lord Jesus, when he put on our feet the glass slipper of salvation. Now we do not live in fear of the clock striking midnight. We are forever sons of God, children of the light.

A man whose identity is in Christ realizes that the model for manhood is not Rambo—with a machine gun in one hand and a belt of bullets around his waist. No, he recognizes that our true model is a carpenter whose hands were stretched on a cross, who chose to sacrifice himself rather than fight back—because that was the greater good.

A man who is not caught in the Hero Image Double Bind lives life with the attitude that he has absolutely nothing to prove. He does not always have to fight or win. He can walk away because he knows he may win the battle if not the war. A man who is not stuck in the Hero Image Double Bind has a *holistic* mindset.

There are two type of thinkers: task-oriented and holistic. The goal of the task-oriented person is to just get the job done, and as a result, this person usually has tunnel vision and blocks everything or everyone out in order to reach his goal. There is a story about Reggie Jackson, the baseball player, when he was playing for the Baltimore Orioles under Earl Weaver. Earl made it clear that his ballplayers were not to steal base without receiving the specific signal to steal. Apparently Reggie had other ideas. He was on first base and decided to steal without Earl's permission. He stole second base but in doing so he completely messed up the overall strategy of the game, because the next batter up was Hal McRae, the Orioles' leading hitter. The pitcher walked Hal McRae and pitched to the next batter, who was a poor hitter and hit into a double play ending the inning. If Reggie had allowed their best hitter, McRae, to hit they might have advanced further or even scored. But because of Reggie's move, he took the bat out of McRae's hands. That is how a task-oriented thinker works: they live life to get only to the next level but do not see the broader implications of reaching that level.

The other type is called the holistic thinker. This type of person thinks in terms of *who* will be affected if they follow a certain course of action. They think in terms of relationships and the overall consequences to those around them. I remember a friend of mine in seminary named Joe who lived life holistically. He was married and had two children, three and five years of age. Seminary was competitive. I was always amazed at how anxiously we waited at our mailboxes in the student lounge to receive our grades after a test. Immediately, we compared test scores. I notice that Joe, however, never got into this sort of competition, so I asked him why. He said that he remembered something that Howard Hendricks once said in class, and he wanted to live by it. Joe explained, "Hendricks said, 'You didn't make a vow to this seminary, gentlemen—you made a vow to your wife. Make sure your books go up on the shelf—not your wife and children.' From that point on I made some decisions. I determined that getting B's and C's was okay as long as I got A's in marriage and fathering. You see, Rod, nobody's going to invite me into ministry if I got an A in Hebrew, but they sure are going to look at my family and children and grade me in relationships." Joe was a holistic thinker.

Finally, if a man is going to stay out of the Hero Image Double Bind he must remember to take care of himself physically and emotionally. A good warrior does not fight out of his deficits but out of his strengths. So how does a warrior stay strong?

1. Down Time Is Extremely Important

What do you do for yourself to recover and renew yourself? It is extremely important that you take the time to be refreshed.

2. Chart Your Emotional Landscape

Imagine you are an explorer observing and discovering a new land called Emotions. Begin by making an hour-by-hour chart of the range of emotions you experience and express on an average day. What do you feel like when you wake up? Do you anticipate the day with excitement or dread? Do your dreams inspire you with fear, anxiety, or hopefulness? What emotions dominate your workday? Frustration? Satisfaction? Resentment? Numbness? Creative joy? Boredom? Fatigue? What do you feel when you go home? Loneliness? Relief? Contentment? Begin to get feeling checks so you are aware and can begin to deal with your feelings as they happen rather than waiting for them to explode.

3. Tell Someone You Trust about Your Observations

Just talking about it will begin to show you that you are normal. I would encourage you to share with another man or a small group of men. Also, do not share your emotions with another woman. Those types of alliances can lead to affairs if you are not careful—so I recommend against it. Also, if you have some specific struggles, say with pornography or lust, share first with your friends. When you have their support and encouragement, then pray about when and if you should share this with your wife.

4. Finally, Say This Prayer (by Joe Bailey)

> Lord of reality, make me real,
> not plastic, synthetic, pretend, phony,
> an actor playing out his part, hypocrite.
> I don't want to keep a prayer list
> but to pray.
> Nor agonize to find your will
> but to obey what I already know.
> I don't want to argue theories of inspiration
> but submit to Your Word.
> I don't want to explain the difference between eros, phileo, and agape
> but to love.

I don't want to sing as if I mean it,
I want to mean it.
I don't want to tell it like it is
but to be like you want it.
I don't want to think another needs me
but I need him else I'm not complete.
I don't want to tell others how to do it
but to do it.
I don't want to have to be always right
but to admit it when I'm wrong.
I don't want to be a census taker
but an obstetrician.
Nor an involved person, a professional,
but a friend.
I don't want to be insensitive
but to hurt where other people hurt.
Nor to say I know how you feel
but to say God knows, and
I'll try if you'll be patient with me,
and meanwhile I'll be quiet.
I don't want to scorn the clichés of others
but to mean everything I say—including this.[4]

DISCUSSION QUESTIONS

1. Define *protection*. Where did you learn this definition? Does
   it need to be changed in any way? Why or why not?
2. What is the difference between a warrior and a soldier?
3. Are you a holistic or task-oriented thinker?
4. How does your identity in Christ effect your role as a protector?

CHAPTER 6

What's Going On in There Anyway?

Not long ago, I was the master of ceremonies at a Promise Keepers event in Houston, Texas, where approximately 43,000 had come to learn how to be better husbands, fathers, friends—in essence, better men. On that Friday evening, I went to the hotel restaurant to get some dessert. It had been a long day and we had just finished up the evening meetings. At the counter, the waitress asked me for my order. Noticing the Promise Keepers logo on my shirt, she asked, "What's going on in there anyway?" She was curious to know what would bring 43,000 men together without a sporting event being involved. "Look," she said, "what are you guys *really* up to? I mean, can 43,000 men get together just to worship God, like you said? And let me ask you this—why all *men*? Why not couples? Can't you do what you need to do with your wives present?"

Good questions.

I proceeded to explain that men have been far too dependent on women to meet their needs and now need to build relationships with other men—men who would hold them directly accountable and thereby take some of the pressure off their wives.

The waitress then said, "But I thought a *wife* was to be her husband's best friend."

I acknowledged that she was correct, but I also pointed out that a wife couldn't be a man's *only* friend. In fact, I told her, there are some things that only a man can give another man, such as a sense of "blessing" and the support of a team to help him through tough times. I also said that there are some issues a man feels most free in telling another man—experiences only a man can identify with—just as there are issues that a woman can only tell another woman.

The waitress still was not convinced. She still thought something "fishy" was going on with all of these men meeting together without their wives. Why? Why was this woman so distrustful? What was she afraid was *really* going to happen when these guys went home?

At that same conference, I was a part of the press conference team with the president of Promise Keepers, Randy Phillips, and co-founder, Coach Bill McCartney. We met with a group of reporters, who came with their notepads and cameras on tripods and their floodlights that lit up the room—all to record the rapid fire action of questions and answers. One reporter, who happened to be a woman, said, "What do you teach about women in these conferences?"

Coach McCartney said, "We teach men that they should cherish, honor, and support their wives in every way."

She then asked, "But aren't you *really* teaching men to dominate their wives and make them submit?"

Coach McCartney, turning a little red, said, "Why don't you trust us? We do not have a hidden agenda. We just want to help men to be better men at home, at work, or wherever they happen to be. In fact, stay and listen—you will see we have nothing to hide."

I believe that the reporter and the waitress had a hard time dealing with men getting together with men because of something I call the Companionship Double Bind.

The Companionship Double Bind

Most parents would be deeply concerned if their young son preferred the company of females. A young boy is therefore encouraged to play primarily with other boys, to participate in masculine activities and stay away from "playing house." Yet when he becomes an adult, the exact opposite is expected of him. If he prefers companionship with other males, he could be labeled a homosexual. As a married man, he must learn to enjoy "playing house," and he must consider his wife as his primary (often times only) companion and friend. He is to make her an integral part of his leisure-time activities.

Either Way He Loses

As an adult, if a man behaves in a way that is consistent with his early experiences, he will be seen as immature, rejecting, hostile to women, latently homosexual, or chauvinistic. If he behaves in the way that is expected of him, he will do it at the price of denying himself an intrinsic source of pleasure (men need men to receive the blessing). Caught in this bind, a man may become passive-aggressive—that is, he won't do the things he really wants to do ("Gee, will it be worth catching hell from my wife over this?"), but he also won't get into and fully enjoy activities with his wife. Instead, he will function in a relatively detached, passive manner, sitting at home or elsewhere doing nothing. He won't please himself or his spouse.

Early on, men and women are taught that a man should look exclusively to his wife for all his nurturing. Though not spoken verbally, this assumption is taught socially. This, I believe, is why women become so frustrated and men become so angry in a marriage. A woman can only give so much—she cannot be an infinite source of support. In fact, the Companionship Double Bind puts the woman in a serious bind as well because she now must be everything to the man.

I do not believe that marriage is intended to support the notion that one person should be an inexhaustible source of nurture for another. If that notion were true, then why would we need God? Out of frustration, therefore, a woman reads romance novels, goes back to school, or gets a job—just to get some nurturing for herself. This in turn makes the man feel threatened because she finds satisfaction in other activities besides him and may spend less time with him. As a result, he loses his only source of emotional support and nurture, since chances are he has no deep friendships—especially with other men. As a result, many men feel powerless emotionally and relationally because they have relegated those aspects of their lives to their wives.

A man usually makes his wife his sole source of emotional support.

Something else also keeps both men and women locked in the Companionship Double Bind: the Autonomy Double Bind.

The Autonomy Double Bind

Usually, a man is encouraged to be independent and *not* to lean on others for help. If he does lean on others, it is usually only his wife, and then only to a degree. Otherwise, a man is supposed to be autonomous. However, a man still has a deeply rooted need to be nourished and cared for.

Either Way He Loses

If he resists asking for the help, care, or nurture he desires, he will suffer alone in silence, exhausted, torturing himself, fighting uphill battles, and draining his energies in the process. If he asks for help and allows himself to be dependent (even on his wife), he becomes anxious, uncomfortable, and feels vulnerable. If he admits to being confused, lost, or troubled, he feels his masculinity is at stake.

As Herb Goldberg wrote in his book *The New Male:* "To be strong, the prisoner once wrote, a man 'must be able to stand utterly alone, able to meet and deal with life relying solely upon his own inner resources.' To show he was such a man, he once held his hand over a candle flame without flinching. This is G. Gordon Liddy."[1]

I would like to think that G. Gordon Liddy is an aberration. But when it comes to the idea that a man must be autonomous—stand alone and be tough—many men believe and practice what Liddy espouses. As a popular deodorant commercial says, "Never let them see you sweat."

John Gray, in his book *Men Are from Mars and Women Are from Venus,* makes an excellent observation: "Autonomy is a symbol of efficiency, power, and competence. . . . To offer a man unsolicited advice is to presume that he doesn't know what to do or that he can't do it on his own. Men are very touchy about this, because the issue of competence is so very important to them. . . . Asking for help when you can do it for yourself is perceived as a sign of weakness."[2]

Yet as a man grows older he begins to recognize he no longer has the energy he once had to do it "all by himself." Pat Morley, in *The Seven Seasons of a Man's Life,* says, "If I were limited to making only one observation about men today, it would be that everywhere I go I find that men are tired. And I don't mean just physically tired, although that too. But I find that men are mentally, emotionally, psychologically, and spiritually tired. Exhausted by life. Worn to a thread. Beat up. Bone tired."[3]

After a while, when a man reaches forty or so, he begins to run out of energy; he is no longer able to keep up the façade. There appears to be a gradual decline over the years and eventually a man must face the reality that he cannot make it alone. Herb Goldberg gives us a glimpse of some of the stages of decline in a man's life starting at age twenty. Let's take a look at some of them.

1. Restless, passionate about his ideas, eager to push the limits and experiences of his life at twenty, to conservative, "appropriate" and accepting of "reality thirty"; to holding on tight and just trying to maintain his place at forty.

2. Physically active, energetic and finding pleasure in movement and play at twenty, to exercising purposefully in order to fight his waistline and stay in shape at thirty, to engaging in physical

activity at forty, if at all, in a compulsive, serious and measured way, motivated by fear of heart attacks and other physical ailments.

3. Playful, curious, adventurous, and hungry for pleasure at twenty, to controlled, with his pleasure outlets limited to dinners out, movies, television, photography, and shopping at thirty, to passive and reluctant to try new things or to forsake the sporting event on television at forty.

4. Buddyship oriented and close to male friends who are important to him at twenty, to being more guarded around other men and getting together socially usually only in the company of wives or girlfriends at thirty, and at forty in a situation where friendships have evaporated because the men are either divorced, overburdened or living elsewhere and without time or motivation to participate in any close male relationships.

5. Blunt and honest often to the point of rudeness at twenty, to appropriately tactful, phony and manipulative at thirty, to not really knowing what he believes at forty, because everything has by now been discolored by his overriding motivations of expediency and proving himself.[4]

In his forties, a man usually must make a decision. This time in a man's life is usually called a "midlife crisis." I choose to call it a "midlife transition." This stage only becomes a crisis if a man continues to go along with the myth that he can do it "all by myself." If he takes the route of "all by myself" he will end up destroying himself and those around him because he increasingly finds that he has driven everyone away and is literally *all by himself*. If he chooses to ask for help, admit his dependence on others, he can recover.

But we must ask this question: Why are men so stubbornly independent and why are women so willing to nurture men to their own detriment? What happened to cause a woman to be so dependent and a man so independent? The Bible clearly answers this question.

THE ORIGINAL BIND

Genesis 1:26–27 states: "God said, 'Let us make man in our image, in our likeness: and let them rule over the fish of the sea and the birds of the air, over the livestock, and over all the earth, and over all the creatures that move along the ground.' So God created man in his own image, in the image of God he created him; male and female he created them."

Before the Fall (Genesis 3), we find several characteristics common to both the man and the woman in the garden. They were both made in the "image of God," that is, they mirrored God in their ability to think, communicate, and create. They were also both social beings. If God is a trinity, and his image is in all persons, then it comes as no surprise God thought it was "not good" for a man to be alone. So God created woman. God's desire was for man and woman to be interdependent in their relationship to one another. Like God, both men and women are intrinsically social; they are wired for interdependent relationships.

Another common characteristic was that both men and women were given dominion over the rest of creation. They were told, according to Genesis 1:28, to "be fruitful and increase in number; fill the earth and subdue it ... rule over every living thing." At this point there are those who argue over the issue of a man's "headship." I agree that there are certain responsibilities that a man is called to in regards to his wife and his family—he is to protect his family as well as provide an atmosphere conducive to bring out the best in his wife and his children.

But notice this: these verses do not imply that the woman is to be passive. She is right there, along side the man, ruling with him before the Fall. They have a mutual dependence upon one another. Before the Fall, they "submitted to one another" (Eph. 5:21). The man did not lead with an iron fist but with a velvet glove. He was truly a sacrificial servant-leader soliciting his wife's help in the process. You might say they were in a partnership.

But then the Fall happened. That event introduced the incredible tension that exists today in men and women—as well as *between* men and women. I call this the Original Bind. After both Adam and Eve willingly violated God's command to not eat of the Tree of Knowledge of Good and Evil, God spoke a series of pronouncements—curses, actually—to discipline Adam and Eve concerning their roles. Genesis 3:16 is of particular interest because it impacts men's and women's relationships. God says to Eve, "I will greatly increase your pains in childbearing; with pain you will give birth to children. Your desire will be for your husband, and he will rule over you."

That last phrase has caused incredible tension between men and women today. Let me try to explain. The phrase "your desire shall be for your husband" seems to connote a woman's longing for intimacy and closeness with her husband, for what they had as a couple before the Fall. But she cannot have it. The other part of the phrase, "but he shall rule over you," seems to imply that the intimacy she desires will not be reciprocated by her husband. Instead of meeting her desire he will rule over her. In other words, the woman wants a soul mate but she gets a master; she wants him to love her but he wants to be lord; she wants to be close but he wants control. Sound familiar? I see it all of the time between men and women today when they come to me for counseling. The woman constantly complains of the need for romance and intimacy while the husband complains that his wife is too smothering and will not give him enough room. It is my belief that on the one hand, as a result of the Fall there was built into men the propensity to dominate and control. God, before the Fall, wanted man to have responsible dominion, which means making decisions in light of all involved. After the Fall, man took that part of the image and it became distorted in that now man wants to dominate. On the other hand, women have the propensity to avoid the loss of a relationship at any cost. Her tremendous desire for closeness causes her to stuff who she is in order to win his approval and somehow attain intimacy, but his fear is of her controlling him if he lets her too close so he keeps her at arm's length.

The effects of Genesis 3:16 reflect the peculiar way in which each party sinned. The man and the woman were equally created for relationship and intimacy and dominion. But on the one hand, in eating the fruit, the woman overstepped the bounds of accountable dominion to her husband and to God. As a consequence, her desire for relationship became magnified to the point that she would rather take abuse and have some sort of relationship than have no relationship at all.

On the other hand, the man, in accepting the fruit from his wife, instead of speaking up and setting a boundary by being a leader, overstepped the bounds of responsibility to maintain unity. As a result, on the one hand, his desire for dominion turned into an obsession for control and thus domination. This instilled in him a tremendous and fierce independence that has interfered with his relationships—to God, to his wife and family, and to others, especially other men.

On the other hand the woman has so sacrificed herself for relationship that eventually she gets fed up and looks for other avenues of being nurtured because of the tremendous autonomy in men. Men and women suffer greatly because of the effects of the Fall. But thank God—there is an answer to this bind.

It Shall Not Be So Among You

It was a simple request. It was a *big* request but a simple one. At least that is how the mother of Zebedee's sons, James and John, saw it. All this mother wanted was for her sons to sit on either side of Jesus when he came into his kingdom. Like I said, a simple request. But the other disciples were angry—probably because they hadn't thought of it first. But notice Jesus' response. It was not blame and shame but one of responsibility. "Can you drink the cup I am going to drink?" (Matt. 20:22). Good question. But Jesus then goes on to mark out what will be different about *his* disciples when it comes to leadership from the world's definition of leadership. Jesus says, "You know that the rulers of the Gentiles lord it over them, and their high officials exercise authority over them. Not so with you. Instead, whoever wants to become great among you must be your servant, and whoever wants to be first must be your slave—just as the Son of Man did not come to be served, but to serve, and to give his life as a ransom for many" (Matt. 20:25–26).

Notice that Jesus says that what distinguishes his disciples' leadership style from the world's is that they do not "lord" it over others. In other words, they no longer need to *dominate* to keep control; instead, they are to be *servants*. Man, what a change. This not only applies to leadership in the community but also in marriage. Listen to Ephesians 5:25–30:

Husbands, love your wives, just as Christ loved the church and gave himself up for her to make her holy, cleansing her by the washing with water through the word, and to present her to himself as a radiant church, without stain or wrinkle or any other blemish, but holy and blameless. In this same way, husbands ought to love their wives as their own bodies. He who loves his wife loves himself. After all, no one ever hated his own body, but he feeds and cares for it, just as Christ does the church—for we are members of his body.

Notice that the man is no longer interested in keeping control, but *his* desire is to have intimacy and a close relationship. This breaks the Original Bind. No longer does his wife have to relentlessly pursue intimacy because her husband desires it as much as she. On the other hand, Ephesians 5:22–24 says,

Wives, submit to your husbands as to the Lord. For the husband is the head of the wife as Christ is the head of the church, his body, of which he is the Savior. Now as the church submits to Christ, so also wives should submit to their husbands in everything.

A wife no longer needs to smother her husband or give up who she is to please him because *he* cherishes *her* for the gift she is to him. But none of this can happen without the transforming work of Jesus Christ in both the man's and woman's life. The husband no longer has to dominate, and the wife no longer needs to smother because they are now channels of blessing and no longer reservoirs of selfishness. They look to God who then enables them to fulfill the partnership he intended before the Fall.

A man's identity in Christ now frees him up to love openly and not put up walls around himself. His relationship in Christ allows him to be "naked and not ashamed," because he now no longer has anything to hide—God has seen him at his worst and says, "I am still with you my child." He has nothing to prove—the One who loves him the most has granted approval. He has nothing to lose—he can give his all to his wife and friends without fear because he is now a channel of God's grace regardless of their responses.

So what must a man do to keep this perspective in his relationships and not get caught in the Companionship Double Bind and the
Autonomy Double Bind? I'm glad you asked.

NO LONE RANGER CHRISTIANS

The Europeans who settled North America found it vast and
unexplored. "Self-reliance" was the watchword, and the scout, the
mountain man, and the pioneer, with an ax and a rifle over his shoulder, became the national hero.

In those early days the government gave away quarter sections of
land to anyone who would homestead them, to encourage settlement.
People flocked west from crowded cities and villages to have their own
land at last. Before they could farm the land, though, they had to build
a sod hut to live in, and we know that most families built them right
smack dab in the middle of their quarter section. The reason was obvious. People who had never owned land before had a new sense of pride
and ownership. They wanted to feel that everything they saw belonged
to them.

But that custom changed very quickly. This chosen isolation did
strange things to people. Occasionally, photographers went out to
record life on the frontier and returned with photographs of weird
men, wild-eyed women, and haunted looking children. Before long,
most of these families learned to move their houses to one corner of
their property. Four families living together—sharing life and death,
joy and sorrow, abundance and want—had a good chance of making it.

Bruce Larson, in his book *There Is a Lot More to Health than Not
Being Sick*, points out that unhappy and unhealthy things happen to us
when we isolate ourselves from one another. Those families on the
plains learned that isolation can cause great harm. Only in community
can we face the storms of life and stay afloat.

The same is true for men. Nowhere in the Bible is isolationism
condoned. From Genesis to Revelation, those whom God calls his
people are to be in communion with him and each other. David had
Jonathan, Jesus had the Twelve. In fact, when Jesus sent his disciples

out on a mission he always sent them in groups of two or more. There is no such thing as a Lone Ranger Christian in God's economy.

The tragedy is that so few men—even Christian men—have experienced the friendship of other men on a deep level. I have found that most men past the age of thirty do not have real friends. They have colleagues, work buddies, golf buddies, and maybe a "couple" friend where the bond is really between the wives. If a man does say he has a best friend it often turns out to be an old friend whom he may see or speak to every few months—even years. Why do men fail to connect on that "friendship" level? Simply put—our culture discourages it. In fact our culture discourages male friendship in three ways.

1. Men Are Not to Have Any Emotional Needs

Larry Letich, in his article, "Do You Know Who Your Friends Are?" says,

> If a man manages to have any true emotional attachment to another man you will find a lot of subtle pressures to eliminate it. The most obvious time this happens is when a man gets married (especially if he is still in his twenties). Think of the impression that comes to mind from a thousand movies and TV shows about the guy who "leaves his wife" for the evening to "go out with the guys." Invariably, the other guys are shown as both immature and lower-class, losers who'll never amount to anything in life. The message is clear—no self-respecting middle-class man hangs out regularly with his friends.
>
> In fact, friendship between men is rarely spoken of at all. Instead, we hear something called male bonding, as if all possible non-sexual connection between men is rooted in some crude, instinctual impulse. More often than not, male bonding is sniggered at as something terribly juvenile and possibly dangerous.[5]

Sounds like the Companionship Double Bind, doesn't it? A man who has any other important emotional bonds (not based on duty, such as an ailing parent) is in danger of being called neglectful, irresponsible, or weak, because forging bonds with others takes time that is supposed to be spent with family and also with getting ahead. The tragedy is that the church reinforces the idea of being a protector so much that a man's need to depend on others is usually minimized or seen as a luxury not a necessity.

2. Do Not Trust Other Men — They Are Your Competition

In this culture men are encouraged not to trust each other or be together. We are to be constantly and often ruthlessly competing with each other for our "piece of the pie." Friendship requires vulnerability. If I open up to another man, he has the edge and will therefore get ahead. Also, if I share my deepest heart with another man, he may perceive me as weak, and if I am perceived as weak I will be labeled a loser.

3. Normalcy—Pretending That Everything Is Okay

I call it the Let's Spill It Out Syndrome: "Hi—how are you— just fine thanks." Men are great pretenders. If we have disappointments or pain, we have been taught "to take it like a man." Two men will play a game about who they are and how well they are doing when in reality they are dying.

THE FRIENDSHIP FACTOR

Studies have shown that men with at least one close friend in whom they can confide about themselves and their problems have, in effect, a buffer against such crises as the loss of a wife or job, a chronic illness, and the psychological stresses of aging. In terms of their morale and health, these men have a significant edge over men who lack a close confidant.

I mentioned earlier, God never intended for us to go it alone. Jesus, our example, had twelve men around him. They walked together, ate together, lived together. During the most crucial time of Jesus' life, in the Garden of Gesthemane, he called for his closest friends—James, John, and Peter. In his anguish and crying out to God he asked them to pray for him and be there with him. Why? Because these were his *friends*. Jesus, in his humanity, needed their support in that dark hour. Let me ask you a question. If Jesus had a group of men around him for support and encouragement—can you afford not to? That is what I thought—me neither. Let me give you some keys on how to begin to forge good friendships and break the Companionship and Autonomy Double Binds.

1. *It has to become a top priority.* Sounds simple and obvious, but it usually isn't. You have to want it badly enough to work at getting it. Do not let the old messages of our culture convince you that you do not need a strong male friendship. It will help your marriage by taking some of your stresses from work off of your wife and sharing it with your friend. It will help your children by giving them a less stressed-out dad, and it will help you to find out your struggles are normal. Make this a top priority in your life.

2. *Identify a possible friend.* Someone with whom you think will be real and you can feel safe with. Pray about that person then seek him out.

3. *Set aside the time.* It takes time to build trust. Look at a normal week, then carve out an hour or two to schedule a regular time with your friend.

4. *Look for a common interest.* It may be golf, tennis, fishing, or a number of activities. All that matters is that you find some common ground to begin the relationship.

5. *Be on time.* Do not be late for your meetings. Show respect for that other man by showing that he is important enough for you to be there. Being late usually signifies "I am more important than you—that is why I'm late." Do not be late.

6. *Persist.* Keep planning and going. If you want a friend you may have to do the pursuing 80 percent of the time at first. Breaking the Autonomy Double Bind takes time and persistence.

7. *Honor confidences and secrets.* Private matters shared in confidence must remain so. Do not share with others, even for prayer purposes, what you have discussed with your friend.

8. *Practice Openness.* Open up your life a little bit at a time with one another. Every time you get together with your friend try to reveal at least one new significant thing about yourself. Your openness will begin to earn you the right to ask your friend to be open as well.

During the 1992 Olympics, Ivan Maisel of the *Dallas Morning News* described a touching moment between a father and a son who were also good friends. He wrote:

> Jim Redmond did what any father would do. His child needed help. It was that simple. "One minute I was running," Derek Redmond of Great Britain said, "The next thing I heard a pop. I went down."
>
> Derek, at 26, had waited for this 400 hundred meter semifinal for at least four years. In Seoul, he had an Achilles' tendon problem. He waited until a minute and a half before the race began before he would admit he couldn't run.
>
> Now in Barcelona, halfway around the track, Redmond lay sprawled across lane 5. "It dawned on me I was out of the Olympic Final," he said. "I just wanted to finish that race."
>
> Redmond struggled to his feet and began hobbling around the track. The winner of the heat, defending Olympic champion Steve Lewis, had finished and headed toward the tunnel. So had the other six runners. But the last runner in the heat hadn't finished. He continued to run.
>
> Jim Redmond (Derek's dad), sitting high in the stands at Olympic stadium, saw Derek collapse. "You don't need accreditation in an emergency," Redmond said. So Redmond ran down the steps (past security guards) and onto the track. "I was thinking," Jim Redmond said, "I had to get him there so he could say he finished the semifinal."
>
> The crowd realized that Derek Redmond was running the race of his life. Around the stands, fans from around the world stood and honored him with cheers.
>
> At the final turn, Jim Redmond caught up to Derek and put his arm around his son. Derek leaned on his dad's right shoulder and sobbed. But they kept going. An usher attempted to intercede and escort Jim Redmond off the track. If ever a futile mission had been undertaken . . .
>
> They crossed the finish line, father and son, arm in arm.[6]

You and I are in a race. Sometimes, due to the pressures of life, we can pop a hamstring physically, emotionally, spiritually, and even psychologically. Who do you have in the stands to come and help you finish the race when you fall down? Remember, "Two are better than one, because they have a good return for their work: If one falls down, his friend can help him up. But pity the man who falls and has no one to help him up" (Ecc. 4:9–10).

Friendship is like high grade fuel—it takes the knock out of living.

DISCUSSION QUESTIONS

1. Do you dominate or empower those around you? If you empower, how? If you dominate, how?
2. Do you have a close male friend? If yes—how has it helped? If not—why not?
3. Are you tired? Finish the phrase, "I am tired of _____ _____." List as many things as you can.
4. How does my identity in Christ and inclusion in the body of Christ free me up as a man?

CHAPTER 7

I'm Just A-Passin' Through

I was restless. I needed to make a decision concerning my ministry. I was just finishing my Ph.D. in counseling and had several opportunities. One was to go to a Christian college and become the head of the counseling department. The other was for me to become the pastor of family ministries in a church where I would also start a small group ministry, among other responsibilities.

On my vacation I sat down with a key mentor in my life, Joe Wall. As an ordained minister, he married my wife, Nancy, and me. He also placed me in my first ministry as the director of the Houston Bible Institute. I asked him, "Which career path do you think would be most advantageous for ministry?"

Joe thought for a moment and said, "Rod, when it comes to Christian ministry—there is no such thing as a career path." I asked what he meant. He explained that in the Christian life there are "upward moves, lateral moves, or downward moves." The important thing was to be in a position where God could use me effectively.

I countered by saying, "But aren't I responsible to use my gifts to their fullest potential?"

"Yes," said Joe, "but *where* they are to be used is up to God. You may be a professor in a school or you may be a pastor in a small church

103

or you may even do private practice as a counselor. Your job is to develop your gifts and be available—it is God's job to place you—wherever that may be."

I must admit that I struggled with Joe's answer, not because of its content but because of a key implication that really got my attention and eventually set me *free*.

HE IS LORD

I discovered that God might choose something different for me than I envisioned. I mean, who does God think he is anyway—God? Joe lovingly showed me that in the Christian life there are no upward or downward moves—there are only God moves.

I was looking at the ministry from the Career-Ladder Double Bind mentality. I knew all of the Christian lingo about service and ministry, but in reality I did not want to pastor a small church or be unable to climb the ladder of what I envisioned as "successful ministry." I figured I could have my earthly cake and eat my spiritual cake too. I do not recall anyone in seminary clambering to stay on as a youth pastor or an assistant pastor. I usually heard those terms being used in the context of getting to the next level, which was being a senior pastor or a professor in seminary. Success, even in the ministry, was getting to the next level. I had great plans for my ministry—I mean, God's ministry. My job was to map the plan out and God's job was to bless it, kind of a partnership. And that is what it was, only I was to be the senior partner. I mean, God would benefit from these plans too, wouldn't he?

Then came Joe, reminding me, in the words of an old black spiritual, that as a man of God (by the way, any man who knows Jesus Christ as his personal savior is a man of God): "This world is not my home—I'm just a-passin' through." He reminded me that God has the right to invade and interrupt my life anytime he wants. He is Lord. When I trusted Jesus Christ as my Lord, I gave *him* the right to help himself to my life anytime he wants.

I came to realize that I had been living by two sets of scriptures: the sacred Scriptures (that is, the Bible, which I believed and gave verbal assent to) and the secular scriptures (the scriptures I actually lived out in my life). I realized that Jesus was right—I could not serve "God and Mammon." There was a conflict between two kingdoms. I unconsciously approached my relationship to God as a partnership. I figured if I did the ministry, went to seminary, and was a good boy I would get rewarded—*should* get rewarded. That was the deal. Now, looking back, I see that I got caught in the Breadwinner and Career-Ladder Double Binds.

But why was I not allowing God to be Lord of my Life? I believe there are three reasons—shall we say "rules"—that make lordship difficult.

THREE RULES FOR MEN

Hang with me here, because I am going to sound like a counselor. I have worked with a lot of families over the years and found that each one has a set of rules to keep order in the home. Rules can be helpful. They also can cause great harm if they are overly rigid. For instance, one woman wanted to teach her daughter a lesson for her misbehavior. The daughter was about five at the time. The mother sat her daughter down and pulled out a letter size piece of paper. She then drew a circle on the paper and drew lines through the circle so it appeared like a pie that had been sliced. The mother then said to her daughter, "Now honey, every time I color in one of these slices it means that you have been bad. And, if and when I color in all of the slices of the pie, it means that God doesn't love you anymore." Did you catch that? "God doesn't love you anymore"! Whatever the mother's intention, the daughter really learned the following things from this overly severe rule:

1. Do not cause conflict.
2. Do not make other people unhappy or you will lose their approval.
3. Always perform to their expectations.
4. God's love is conditional.

5. Do not say or feel or do anything that would make God or Mom angry.

Wow—quite a list! This prepared the little girl to live her life in a performance mode, not to be authentic in what she felt or thought. It taught her that appearance is more important than substance.

Sound familiar? I believe that by putting men in the "man box," society has given men three rules.

Rule One: Do Not Trust

If self-reliance is key for men, then we are by no means to depend on anyone. Competition breeds distrust. If it is "every man for himself," then there is no way that I am going to be vulnerable or let anyone in. Men are taught that relationships require performance. If there is a relationship, it is because you want something from me. For instance, I have found that women *do* lunch just to be with each other. There is no particular reason to get together outside of the fact that they just want to get together. Men must come up with pragmatic reasons to *do* lunch. I have purposely asked men to go to lunch and refused to give them a reason. When we would meet at the restaurant I would time how long it would take them to ask me, "Okay, Rod, what do you want?"

Men only connect when they want to advance their goals. If there is no obvious agenda, then the search is on for a hidden agenda. Men are taught not to trust. Add to that the need to perform, and a *quid pro quo* mentality begins: I do something for you—you do something for me in return.

How do you think such a rule affects a man's relationship with God? Men often think: God wants to be with me because he wants something from me—not *me*—but something *from* me. You mean, God just wants to be with me? Come on—what's the catch? Hey, I believe in grace (per sacred Scripture), but I still have to get my righteousness the old fashioned way—I earn it (per secular scripture).

Men have a hard time with lordship because we are not sure what God is *really* after, so we do not trust him, and we hold back, waiting to see how much God wants.

Rule Two: Do Not Feel

We have already said a lot on this issue but suffice it to say a man must not let feelings get in the way. Emotions are essential for relationships with God. Emotions are an essential part of worship, for instance. David danced before the Lord. He was passionate about his God. Yet men today are supposed to be passionless. Men are taught to "take it like a man—numb it out." Listen to this anonymous poem:

What is this big, dark, empty hole in the middle of my chest? This voracious cavity that sucks everything in that is not tied down, vainly attempting to be filled. Years and years of mindless activity. Alcohol, drugs, sex, money, work, things, anything so I don't have to look at this hole in the middle of my chest.

It is sad and lonely, so I attract others; usually inappropriate others. It is empty, so I seek to be filled; usually with inappropriate things. It is full of pain, so I seek to be soothed; in all the wrong ways. It is full of fear, so I am given to ego and pride, bravado and boasting; so others won't know. It is festering anger; I lash out at the innocents around me, confounding myself.

When I listen; It's voice is a wailing moan in the deep, dark, recesses of my being. When I feel; It is a burning in my solar plexus that will not be cooled; it is emptiness that will not be filled. It is profound sadness. It is my human spirit, my soul, longing for oneness with God that my humanness for so long has denied.

Only a hug; just a kiss; one more drink; a bigger paycheck; some more of that white stuff; another man; another woman; one more deal; a faster car; a bigger bike ... NO! ... NO! ... NO GOD! ... YOU![1]

Rule Three: Do Not Talk

Talking requires vulnerability, which leads to intimacy. I have found there are five levels of intimacy.

Level One is what I call "weather channel intimacy." It is shallow and superficial. It is when I say, "Gee, this day is beautiful" and that is it.

Level Two is when I venture out to give you an opinion about how the weather is *affecting* me. I might say, "This rain really depresses me." Still shallow but a little insight into me.

Level Three is when I dare to give an opinion about something with which you might disagree. I become vulnerable. I might say, "I do not like the health care plan" or something similar. This is moving toward more commitment and trust.

But true intimacy does not take place until I get to *Levels Four* and *Five*. These levels happen at the point at which the person I am sharing with feels free to share their own hopes, dreams, fears, and failures with me, and I can do the same with them. It is emotional, deep and personal.

I find most men have a hard time getting beyond Level Three because it requires vulnerability and *talking* about things. I have already said that men do not really share how they feel because they might be seen as a loser. I believe men shy away from prayer for the same reason. It requires openness and vulnerability, and I do not want God to disapprove of how I feel about life—and maybe even about *him*. These rules cause many men to stay away from the lordship of Christ. So what must happen for a man to "surrender"?

I SURRENDER ALL BECAUSE . . .

God is so good,
God is so good,
God is so good,
He's so good to me.

Do you recognize it? I am sure you do. I don't know how many times I have sung that chorus mindlessly, but there is a lot of theology in it. God is *good.* The word means "one who is superior, excellent in character, always doing the right thing." God is good. That means that "God works for the good of those who love him, who have been called according to his purpose" (Rom. 8:28).

Now you might say, "If God is good, then why did I lose my job? Why did I get cancer? Why can't I get ahead? Why did my marriage fail?" As I've mentioned before, the word *good* in Romans 8:28 is further defined in verse 29 as whatever helps us become "conformed to the likeness of his Son." Listen to the apostle Paul in 2 Corinthians 4:16–18:

> Therefore we do not lose heart. Though outwardly we are wasting away, yet inwardly we are being renewed day by day. For our light and momentary troubles are achieving for us an eternal glory that far outweighs them all. So we fix our eyes not on what is seen, but on what is unseen. For what is seen is temporary, but what is unseen is eternal.

My friend, you will not surrender to Christ and break the binds of life if you do not believe in the fundamental fact that *God is good* and his intentions toward you are only the best.

Max Anders tells a powerful story which shows the goodness of God.

> A number of years ago, the *USS Pueblo,* a ship from the United States Navy, was hijacked by the North Korean military. The incident provoked a tense diplomatic and military standoff for a number of days. The eighty-two surviving crew members were taken into a period of brutal captivity. In one particular instance thirteen of the men were required to sit in a rigid manner around a table for hours. After several hours, the door was flung open, and a North Korean guard brutally beat the man in the first chair with the butt of his rifle. The next day, as each man sat at his assigned place, again the door was thrown open, and the man in the first chair was brutally beaten. On the third day, it happened again to the same man.
>
> Knowing the man could not survive, the next day, another young sailor took his place. When the door was flung open, the guard automatically beat the new victim senseless. For weeks, a new man stepped forward each day to sit in that horrible chair, knowing full well what would happen. At last the guards gave up in exasperation. They were unable to overcome that kind of sacrificial love.[2]

Jesus sat in the first chair for us—took the blows of death that we deserved—so that we might be with him in eternity. *God is so good.* We can trust him. The rule that says "Do not trust" is now cast aside by the One who is trustworthy.

Once I trust someone I can share my innermost thoughts and feelings and not fear rejection. I can get mad at that person and know we will still be friends when it is all over. I can show my feelings because there is no fear of reprisal. I can do all this because I trust that person.

I remember playing golf with some good friends of mine. I will never forget how one of my buddies was having a really hard time. He just could not hit a good drive off of the tee box with his new driver. Finally, after hitting one more bad drive, he went over to a tree where he forcefully hammered the driver into the tree. The driver splintered into pieces until only the stub of the driver with the head on it was left. He came back and said, "Man, did that feel good! I hope you don't mind." We all affirmed his frustration and went on to finish out the hole. My friend said he felt he could do that with us—because we were his friends no matter what. But the point is that we realized that something more was going on with him than just a bad golf day, and we asked him if he wanted to talk about it. Later, in the club house, he was able to discuss the conflicting emotions in his life at the time. He opened up, and we could open up as well. Such sharing of deep emotion only strengthens friendships—and we set up another golf time for the next week.

Do you feel that way with God? Do you have that kind of friendship with him? If not, I have some good news for you. Listen to this:

> What, then, shall we say in response to this? If God is for us, who can be against us? He who did not spare his own Son, but gave him up for us all—how will he not also, along with him, graciously give us all things? Who will bring any charge against those whom God has chosen? It is God who justifies. Who is he that condemns? Christ Jesus, who died—more than that, who was raised to life—is at the right hand of God and is also interceding for us. Who shall separate us from the love of Christ? Shall trou-

ble or hardship or persecution or famine or nakedness or danger or sword? As it is written, "For your sake we face death all day long; we are considered as sheep to be slaughtered." No in all these things we are more than conquerors through him who loved us. For I am convinced that neither death nor life, neither angels nor demons, neither the present nor the future, nor any powers, neither height nor depth, nor anything else in all creation, will be able to separate us from the love of God that is in Christ Jesus our Lord. (Romans 8:31–39)

Stop right now and shout out to God—"Thank you—you are my friend—I trust you—I release my feelings—all of them to you— and I am glad I can talk to you about anything without fear of judgment or losing your friendship. I surrender all. Amen."

It is good to know that God loves us constantly and always has our best interests at heart—even when we suffer. God's grace was sufficient for Jesus—his grace will be sufficient for us. As a man I can now feel freely and fully because I know that this is not all there is to life. As a man, I can now talk openly and be authentic because God did what he did so we could be in relationship. Like Adam in the garden, I can now be vulnerable and exposed and not be ashamed.

Once I recognize whose I am, I am free to live life as God intended. Listen to Pat Morley's insightful words:

> The Bible says that you have been stamped with the *imago dei,* the image of God, and that he, knit you together in your mother's womb. Acts 17:26 says, "He determined the times set for you and the exact places you should live.…
>
> "You are his most excellent creation. You are the full expression of God's creative genius. God was at his very best when he made you."
>
> What should a man say in response to all of this? Simply this: "I am who I am because of the grace of God. He has made me. I belong to Jesus. I am not my own; I have been bought with a price. I am a slave of Jesus Christ. I should no longer (and by God's conquering grace will no longer) live for myself but for him who died

for me and was raised again. I have been crucified with Christ, and I no longer live. The life I live in the body I live by faith in Him who loved me and gave himself for me. For me to live is Christ; to die is gain" (1 Cor. 6:19–20; 2 Cor. 5:15; Gal. 2:20 and Phil. 1:21).[3]

A man's passion and his purpose is to glorify God in all aspects of his life.

There are two key evidences of a man who is convinced of whose he is.

UNDER NEW MANAGEMENT

An illiterate couple had just been recently saved. The man joined in with the men of the church on a building project. The men wore red shirts while engaged in the building project, so the woman made one for the husband. He came home after the meeting, however, with a look of disappointment on his face because the others had a message printed on their shirts but he did not. His wife, undaunted by her inability to read, sewed three words on his shirt which she copied from a sign in a store window across the street. He wore it to the next meeting and came home bubbling with joy. He said all of the men really liked the inscription because it so aptly described the wonderful change they had seen in his life. It turned out that his wife had written, "Under New Management."

Once a man recognizes he is under new management, he develops what is called a "pilgrim's mentality." The apostle Peter says, "Dear friends, I urge you as aliens and strangers in the world, to abstain from sinful desires, which wage war against your soul. Live such good lives among the pagans that, though they accuse you of doing wrong, they may see your good deeds and glorify God on the day he visits us" (1 Peter 2:11–12).

A free man recognizes that he doesn't own anything but is merely a steward of what God has given to him. His payoff is not in this life. Therefore, he does not get hung up about accumulating possessions. His goal is not to be a reservoir of selfishness but a channel of blessing.

So the first evidence of a man who knows whose he is, is that he is open-handed about the possessions God has entrusted to him while on this planet. A friend of mine put it well when he said, "I have learned to live life with an open hand and not to hold onto anything to tightly. Why? Because it hurts too much to have God pry back my fingers to get to it. So I have learned to live my life with an open hand. That way God can put in and take out whatever he wants—and that way I never miss the blessing."

The second key evidence that shows a man recognizes whose he is has to do with his perspective. He has what is called an "eternal" perspective. A free man knows he has a job to do here, which is to manifest the character of Christ and proclaim the name of Jesus to as many who will listen. He knows that we will enjoy fellowship in heaven—forever. He knows we will worship God in heaven—forever. He also knows that evangelism will not be forever—that is *now*. A free man knows he is here on a mission. He has a short-term objective, but also something to look forward to.

I once read about a missionary couple who had spent their entire lives in Africa. They planted churches and worked among the nationals. They treated the people's diseases, taught them to read, instructed them in farming, building, and social and cultural skills. All the while, they shared with them the gospel of Christ.

When the time came for the couple to retire, they sailed home on a large passenger ship. It just so happened that Teddy Roosevelt had been over in Africa on one of his famous safaris, and as the ship docked in the New York harbor, there was a band playing and crowds were cheering for the president returning from his hunting trip.

The missionaries thought, "This is not fair. The president goes hunting and gets a hero's welcome. We spend our lives in an underdeveloped country, meeting peoples needs and introducing them to Christ, and when we come home, there is no party for us."

At that moment, as if God had been standing there and touched them on the shoulder, a still, small voice said, "Ah, yes, but remember, you are not home yet. You have a great party to look forward to!"

A free man recognizes he is not home yet, the best is yet to come.

Discussion Questions

1. What "rules" did you grow up with in your home? List them. Have they affected the way you live? If so, how? Have they affected your relationship with God? If so, how?

2. Define *lordship*. On a scale of 1 to 10 (with 1 being Christ's minimal lordship in your life and 10 being his maximum lordship), where would you put yourself? What would it take to get you to the next number?

3. What areas of your life do you still need to put under the "management" of Christ?

4. Read the words and then sing the words to the hymn, "I Surrender All" or "Be Thou My Vision."

CHAPTER 8

Hit the Road, Jack

I grew up on a 500-acre farm among the rolling hills of southern Ohio. The closest town was called Greenfield. Our closest neighbor, named John, lived about a mile away. One of the staples of John's farm was the breeding and selling of beef cattle, particularly a stocky, red-and-white steer called Herefords. One year John decided to crossbreed his cattle to produce a meatier, leaner product, so he decided to buy a Charlais bull, a French breed that produced a calf with leaner meat.

He went to the stock auction to find a Charlais bull that suited his budget and needs. After several hours, they showed a Charlais bull that was magnificent, weighing around 2000 pounds, strong, lean, and well suited for John's purposes. So he bid on him and got him, though he paid a hefty price.

John and some of his friends loaded the bull onto the open-roofed truck and headed off to John's farm. Everything went fine until they got to the freeway. Apparently this bull did not like to travel and began to bellow his displeasure. John figured the bull would adjust and calm down as he traveled further, but what happened next, he said, took him totally by surprise. The bull was so upset, he began to pace back and forth in the truck, rocking it from side to side. So John slowed down. But as he was slowing down, the bull yanked loose the ropes that he was tied with and jumped forward over the roof of the truck. John said he had no idea the bull had gotten loose until he saw four hooves go sailing over the hood of his truck.

John said the bull hit the pavement and slid for about twenty feet and then smashed into a guardrail. John stopped the truck and ran to the bull, only to see the bull get up by himself and wobble all over the road as if it had a hangover. John said once he and his friends had settled the bull down again, he wouldn't move; he just stood there in the highway letting out low level moans and groans.

When the police arrived, they had to call in a truck with a crane to lift the bull off the highway and put him back onto John's truck. John got him home and slowly led him out of the truck. This magnificent, expensive breeding machine now looked like a bull who had been in a train wreck. For several days the bull just stood in the lot and moaned and groaned. He was pretty bruised and sore. John had cows that were ready to breed, but at that moment the bull wasn't interested.

John could have gotten mad and depressed, since he had spent a lot of money on the bull. In fact, John said he might have to put the bull to sleep. But instead of getting angry, John named the bull Jack, in honor of the song "Hit the Road, Jack."

Eventually Jack recovered and fulfilled his destiny as a breeding machine. But what impressed me most was John's ability to laugh about his situation. Every time he told the story, we laughed until our sides split, especially when he got to the part about seeing four hooves come over the hood of the truck and he said to his friends, "Did you see what I saw—a flying bull."

Oh, by the way, did I mention that John was a committed Christian who really loves Jesus? Yep—he sure is.

You see, one of the characteristics of a man who has been set free in Jesus—who has been redeemed—is the ability to laugh at himself and his circumstances. I do not mean that he makes a joke about everything and takes nothing seriously. No, I mean he has the uncanny ability to find humor in any situation and not let things get him down. He knows that God's hands hold the future, and nothing comes his way without it first having passed through the hands of a loving God who has his best interests at heart.

This security gives the free man a contagious, playful serenity. He has spontaneity. He can go with the flow. He is the kind of man who, instead of hurting people with sarcasm or biting remarks, encourages wholesome fun so members of his family and his coworkers do not take themselves too seriously. If he hears a good joke about himself that hits the nail on the head, he can laugh at it as heartily as his friends. Humor is what helps him to live with situations that are unpleasant but that he cannot change.

Being able to laugh gives us power and a new perspective. It can help sustain us and provide the strength to get through the most adverse situations. Laughter also presents us with alternate views of our situation and keeps us in balance when our world seems to be coming apart. For instance, after a tree has fallen on your car, putting a sign on it that reads "Compact Car For Sale" may not make the car whole again, but it most certainly will give you a different perspective.

I believe that the most beneficial therapy God has given us is the ability to laugh. It takes away the heaviness of life and restores perspective for the here and now as well as for the future. Let me give you some of the benefits of being able to laugh.

LAUGHTER GIVES US POWER AND PERSPECTIVE

"A cheerful heart is good medicine, but a crushed spirit dries up the bones" (Proverbs 17:22).

"A happy man makes the face cheerful, but heartache crushes the spirit. . . . All the days of the oppressed are wretched, but the cheerful heart has a continual feast" (Proverbs 15:13, 15).

It has been found that in laughter we can transcend our predicaments. We are lifted above our feelings of fear, discouragement, and despair. The ability to laugh at setbacks keeps us from feeling sorry for ourselves. Instead, we feel uplifted, encouraged, and empowered.

In his book *Man's Search for Meaning*, Viktor Frankl speaks of how he used humor to survive his imprisonment in a Nazi concentration camp during World War II. He and another inmate would invent at least one amusing story every day to help them cope with the horrors. Frankl tells of a time when one prisoner pointed to one of the capos (favored prisoners who acted as guards and became as arrogant as the SS men themselves) and said, "Imagine, I knew him when he was only the president of the bank!"[1] Bill Cosby once said, "If you can laugh at it—you can survive it." Somehow adverse circumstances lose their power when we laugh.

I remember counseling one man who was going through a difficult time in his life. He struggled with his marriage and feared being laid off from his job. If that wasn't enough his teenage son was having emotional problems. I have a desk chair in my office that allows me to swivel around on it as well as lean backward. I am able to set an adjustment to control how far back I can lean. Apparently, I had adjusted it to go all of the way back. As my client began to tell me his story, I took notes and leaned back in the chair. When he got to a difficult story about his son, I went past the point of no return and leaned too far back. The chair flipped over. My legs went straight up into the air, and I landed behind the desk.

At first, my client was silent. But then he began to laugh so hard that he fell off of the chair he was sitting on! Once we were both composed, he said that this was the best session he had ever had. Of course, I had planned this as part of my strategy—*not*!!! Laughing in the midst of the crisis seemed to give him a sense of hope—that somehow in the midst of all his problems he was going to make it. He did.

If anybody can laugh, it is a man who is free in Christ because he knows that this is not all there is to life. There is a whole lot more to come. James 1:2 says we should "consider it pure joy . . . whenever you face trials of many kinds." A free man can withstand and even laugh in the midst of his trials because he has an eternal perspective. A free man realizes that God is using every circumstance he encounters to form the character of Christ within him.

LAUGHTER HELPS US ENJOY THE MOMENT

I think it is often just as holy to laugh as to pray . . . or preach . . . or witness. In fact, laughter *is* a witness. Listen to Chuck Swindoll,

> We have been misled by a twisted, unbalanced mind if we have come to think of laughter and fun as being carnal or even questionable. This is one of Satan's sharpest darts and from the looks of long lines on our faces, some of us have been punctured too many times. Pathetic indeed is the stern, somber Christian who has developed the look of an old basset hound through long hours of practice in restraining humor and squelching laughs.
>
> . . . You simply cannot convince me that during thirty-three years as a carpenter and discipler of the Twelve He never enjoyed a long side-splitting laugh. Wouldn't it be refreshing to see a few pictures of Jesus leaning back with his companions, thoroughly enjoying a few minutes of fun with them? Surely that isn't heresy![2]

A friend of mine once gave me a picture of Jesus laughing. He has a huge grin, and he is holding his stomach as if he were letting out a huge belly laugh at something. I think Jesus loved life and even laughed at it. A free man *lives in the present* and *enjoys the moment*. He does not get so wrapped up in the future that he forgets the present. His desire is to seize the moment and milk it for all that it is worth. He knows that the kinds of memories he creates in the present are what he will hold onto in the future . . . and so will his family. Good memories come from laughing together.

There is a story about a father who told his family that he could not go on their annual vacation because he had to stay home and work. But he really loved his family and wanted them to enjoy the summer vacation without him, so he helped them plan a trip and marked out their itinerary. They would load up their Jeep and drive to Colorado. They would camp at various campsites in the beautiful Rocky Mountain state. Each day was carefully arranged—the routes they would drive and the places they would stop. This father planned the whole route, right down to the time they would reach each state when coming home. It is what he did not tell them that made a difference.

The father took off of work (he had planned it all along) and flew to Colorado. He had arranged to be dropped off along the highway he knew his family would be driving that day. With a wide grin, he sat on his sleeping bag and waited for the familiar Jeep to pass—packed with his wife, kids, and full of gear. When he spotted their Jeep he stood up and stepped out onto the shoulder of the road and stuck out his thumb.

The family assumed he was still back at the office working hard—a thousand miles away. I bet they nearly drove off of the road when they saw this guy who looked just like—Dad. The rest of the trip was a time of laughter and joy because Dad was now with them. When he was later asked why he went to all of that trouble just to get in a few days of vacation with his wife and kids, he said, "Well, someday I'm going to be dead. When that happens, I want my wife and kids to say, 'You know, Dad was a lot of fun.'"

A free man laughs and creates memories. Research says that a man's emotional stability determines the emotional stability of his home. If a man is fun to be around, good things happen. A man who knows how to laugh motivates. His attitude takes the sting out of reality.

HE KEEPS THINGS BASIC AND IN PERSPECTIVE

Humor lends us a fresh eye. It is like one of those old-fashioned "either-or" drawings. You hold it one way and you see the picture of a man who is sad. But you turn it around and the man's beard becomes his hair, his mustache becomes his eyebrows, and suddenly the man is smiling—the same picture, but when seen from another angle it looks entirely different. When we can find humor in our upsets, they no longer seem as large or as important as they once did. Humor expands our limited picture frame and gets us to see more than just the problem. It is our sense of humor, as one writer put it, that gives us a "God's-eye-view" of our situation.

A man who knows how to laugh encourages others. He does not ignore the difficulties in life, but he is able to focus on what is left—not what is lost. A man who knows how to laugh draws people to himself because they see in him a quality that is sadly lacking in our world—the ability to enjoy the moment. This becomes a witness to those around him. They will say, "In the midst of difficulties you can still laugh. How?" Then he can say, "Well, let me tell you about a good friend of mine . . . his name is Jesus. . . ."

A MAN WHO CAN LAUGH HAS BALANCE IN HIS LIFE

I am blessed to be married to an incredible woman. Her name is Nancy. She continually struggles with her health. She has had two back surgeries and is a severe asthmatic. She also has a great sense of humor. She said to me one time, "Would you step on my foot so I can forget about my chest hurting?" She and her father have always refused to let her illnesses get them down. Instead, they laugh about them. I used to get really perturbed about that; I thought they were "in denial." I thought they should just face the facts and deal with reality.

I have come to realize, however, that Nancy *is* dealing with reality—what she needed was relief. Her humor gave her that relief. If she had taken my advice and had not laughed about her situation, she would have been continually depressed.

Finally, I am beginning to see the humor in Nancy's struggles . . . and in my own. By being around Nancy I have seen how little I laugh. Too often I have lived—and have seen other Christians live—by a "cut-the-fun" philosophy of life. Quite frankly, this does not bear witness to the cause of Christ. Part of the abundant life is the ability to laugh . . . even when life is tough.

LAUGHTER HAS PHYSICAL BENEFITS

Proverbs 17:22 says, "A cheerful heart is good medicine." It has been shown that men who are cynical or angry tend to be more prone to heart attacks than those with a more positive outlook.

It has often been thought that the major transitions in life—such as divorce, losing a job, getting married, losing a family member—caused the most stress. Research has shown that this is not true. It is the daily, small stresses of life that, if left unchecked, cause the most damage by manifesting themselves in physical disorders, especially in men who tend to be emotional "stuffers." Humor is a good outlet. In fact, you will remember in the popular series, *MASH*, that it was Hawkeye's and Trapper's sense of humor that gave the whole medical unit a good atmosphere in the midst of wartime conditions. Every day as men, we also go out into wartime conditions. It is our ability to laugh that will keep us healthy.

Dr. William Fry Jr. has studied the physical benefits of laughter. He has found that mirthful laughter affects most, if not all, of the major physiologic systems of the human body. When you laugh, your cardio-vascular system is exercised, your heart rate and blood pressure rise, and then fall again. Your heavier breathing creates a vigorous exchange in your lungs and a healthy workout for your respiratory system. Your muscles release tension as they tighten up and relax again. And finally, endorphins can be released into your blood system, creating the same feelings that long distance joggers experience as "runners'" high.

Heavy laughter is much like aerobic exercise. Dr. Fry says that twenty seconds of laughing gives the heart the same workout as three minutes of hard rowing on a rowing machine. A man who laughs is a healthier man!

———⏤◇▸———

I believe that the greatest challenge for a man is not how he deals with his successes but how he deals with his losses. Life is full of loss. Daily we see our dreams delayed or smashed. Daily we have to give up something to keep going. How we handle loss can either make us bitter—or make us better.

A free man can laugh because he knows that:

1. Each adverse experience helps him grow in the character of Christ.
2. This is not all there is to life—this is preparation for the life to come.
3. Each day is a gift from God—so enjoy the gift.

"This is the day the lord has made—let us rejoice and be glad in it!"

How to Be a Man of Laughter

If this is an area of difficulty for you, let me give you some suggestions.

1. *Take an inventory of your speech.* Ephesians 4:24 says, "Do not let any unwholesome talk come out of your mouths, but only what is helpful for building others up according to their needs." How much do you use sarcasm in your speech? How often do you find yourself being cynical? How often are you complaining and grumbling? This will help you to see what kind of atmosphere you are creating around your family and friends.

2. *Start each day with pleasant words.* Make a conscious effort to be pleasant in your remarks and cheerful with your greetings. Lately, I have found that as soon as I get out of bed in the morning I say, "Thank you Jesus for another day—a gift from your hand." This helps remind me that everyone I come into contact with each day is not there by accident. It also reminds me I do not go through any day alone—God is in control. I will get done all that he wants me to and nothing more.

3. *Smile.* I know. I hate it too when someone tells me to smile. But I do not do it enough. There is tremendous power in just a smile.

Antoine de Saint-Exupéry was a fighter pilot who fought the Nazis in World War II and was killed in action. Before the war, he fought in the Spanish Civil War against the fascists. He wrote a fascinating story based on that experience entitled *The Smile (Le Sourire)*.

Saint-Exupéry said that he was captured by the enemy and thrown into a jail cell. He was sure that from the contemptuous looks and rough treatment he received from his jailers he would be executed the next day. He said,

> I became terribly nervous and distraught. I fumbled in my
> pockets to see if there were any cigarettes which had escaped their
> search. I found one and because of my shaking hands, I could

barely get it to my lips. But I had no matches, they had taken those.

I looked through the bars at my jailer. He did not make eye contact with me. After all, one does not make eye contact with a thing, a corpse. I called out to him, "Have you got a light, por favor?" He looked at me, shrugged and came over to light my cigarette.

As he came close and lit the match, his eyes inadvertently locked with mine. At that moment, I smiled. I don't know why I did that. Perhaps it was nervousness, perhaps it was because, when you get very close, it is very hard not to smile. In any case, I smiled. In that instant, it was as though a spark jumped across the gap between our two hearts, our two human souls. I knew he didn't want to, but my smile leaped through the bars and generated a smile on his lips, too. He lit my cigarette but stayed near, looking at me directly in the eyes and continuing to smile.

I kept smiling at him, now aware of him as a person and not just a jailer. And his looking at me seemed to have a new dimension, too. "Do you have kids," he asked.

"Yes, here, here." I took out my wallet and nervously fumbled for the pictures of my family. He, too, took out the pictures of his niños and began to talk about his plans and hopes for them. My eyes filled with tears. I said that I feared that I'd never see my family again, never have the chance to see them grow up. Tears came to his eyes, too.

Suddenly, without another word, he unlocked my cell and silently led me out. Out of the jail, quietly and by back routes, out of the town. There, at the edge of town, he released me. And without another word, he turned back toward the town.

My life was saved by a smile.[3]

There is something about a smile that cuts beneath all our layers and defenses, and causes a connection. It says, "I recognize you—I want to connect to you." Now I am not saying that we should be skipping and jumping around all of the time. But we can smile. A frowning face repels—a cheerful countenance reaches out and attracts. A smile radiates encouragement and even gives a heart connection. Mother Teresa said, "Smile at each other, smile at your wife, smile at your husband, smile at your children, smile at each other—it doesn't matter who it is—and that will help you to grow up in greater love for each other." If anyone has reason not to smile it is Mother Teresa. She works with some of the most tragic cases of human suffering day in and day out. But she still smiles. So can we.

4. *Look for at least one thing each day to find amusement in or laugh about.* I tend to take my golf game too seriously. I wind up in places that I am sure have been unexplored by any other golfer. I used to really get angry and even—yes—throw a club or two or three . . . okay, you get the picture. But I began to realize I needed to make fun to have fun in golf. So when I ended up in some out-of-the-way spot chasing my ball, I would say, "I've always wanted to see what this part of the course looked like" or "Man, am I getting my money's worth today." Not only did the attempts at humor relax me but also those with whom I was playing. Everybody ended up having a better time.

5. *Express at least one honest comment of appreciation or encouragement to someone every day.* Sharing Christ's love lifts the hearts of those that are heavy. Stubbornly stay away from complaining or camping out on somebody else's weaknesses. Ask the Lord to help you to be genuinely interested in others and not so focused on yourself.

Painter Benjamin West tells how he loved to paint as a youngster. When his mother left the house for a few hours, he would pull out the oils and try to paint. One day he pulled out all of the paints and made quite a mess. He hoped to get it all cleaned up before his mother came back, but she came and discovered the mess anyway. What she did next completely surprised him. She picked up his painting and said, "My, what a beautiful painting of your sister!" She gave him a kiss on the cheek and walked away. With that kiss, West says, he became a painter.

Every day you will find that the people around you need to see Jesus. They will make messes. The tendency will be to scold them and say, "Clean it up!" But what they need is a kiss—a kiss of laughter and encouragement. A free man gives that kiss to those around him because he knows it is vital for life and for relationships.

DISCUSSION QUESTIONS

1. When was the last time you had a good laugh? Describe the situation.
2. Do you think Jesus laughed? Why or why not? If you answered yes describe a situation in which you believe he laughed.
3. Read Philippians 2:14–15. On a scale of 1 to 10 (1 being never and 10 being all the time) how often do you find yourself grumbling and complaining?
4. What must you do to lower the complaint level?

CHAPTER 9

Tender and Tough

I tore it up pretty good. My knee was a mess. I had been playing in a pick-up game at our high school. Since I had lost so much weight and was in such good shape, I was now being asked to play on everyone's team.

Around noontime a bunch of us guys would get together to play football. Some of the guys played on the varsity football team. We usually played touch football, but today, since it was only a half day of school, we decided to go all out and play tackle. We didn't worry about keeping our clothes clean since we were not going back to class that afternoon.

My team was ahead by a touchdown. The other team had the ball. They ran a play to my side of the field. The guy carrying the ball had gotten by everyone, and I was our team's last hope in stopping a touchdown. As the runner approached me, I lunged at him and dragged him to the ground. I stopped the touchdown from happening. While my team was rejoicing I could feel something warm and liquidy running down my leg. I looked at my knee and saw blood gushing out of it. I also saw chunks of glass sticking out of it as well. I made the tackle but in dragging the runner down I fell onto the jagged edge of a broken bottle.

My friends rushed me to our family doctor who was only ten minutes from school. They also called my family and my dad showed up.

The doctor came in and stopped the bleeding. He said that he could not use any kind of painkiller to deaden the pain because where he had to stick the needle was where the broken glass was lodged. He would have to remove the glass, buried in my knee, with a pair of tweezers and without painkiller. I knew this was going to hurt. So did my dad.

I looked at the doctor and said, "No way. It's gonna hurt too much."

The doctor said he would have to if my knee was going to be saved. I resisted and started to cry because I knew the pain I was about to face. My dad started to cry too. He too knew the pain I was about to face. My dad also knew this procedure had to occur for my knee to be repaired. So, in an act of love, my dad grabbed me and held me down on the table, while the doctor began his work. I yelled and screamed for my dad to let me up. I said if he loved me he wouldn't let the doctor do this to me.

I said, "It really hurts." I was no wimp—I could take pain, but this was incredible!

My dad said, "Son, I know it hurts, but I love you too much not to hold you down. Just hold onto me—I'm here with you."

The glass was removed and the knee has recovered. I now know my dad did what he did because he loved me—even if it meant I had to hurt for a while. I discovered through that ordeal two key characteristics about a man who is free in Jesus Christ.

A free man can be a *motherly man*—showing tenderness and compassion when someone is hurt. At the same time, he can be a *fatherly man*—showing strength and setting boundaries when needed. Let's take a further look at these two key characteristics.

THE MOTHERLY MAN

I wish to thank Walter Trobisch for coining this term concerning a man's ability to be tender. I have found that when a man is set free in Jesus Christ he no longer has to stifle his emotions. He can now display all facets of who he is because he has been set free indeed by Jesus. Three of the fruits of the Spirit listed in Galatians 5:22–23 are *kindness, goodness,* and *gentleness.* These are incredibly important traits if a man is to show the tenderness of God.

Walter Trobisch, in his book *All a Man Can Be,* gives this example of God's tenderness:

> The Kiga tribe in East Africa gives God the name Biheko, which means, "a God who carries everyone on his back." In this tribe, only mothers and older sisters carry children on their backs while fathers never do. To portray Biheko, one of their artists made a wooden carving portraying a man who carries on his back a child with an adult face and in his arms a weaker child. The carving is a symbol of the God who takes care of human beings with the tender care of a mother.[1]

The whole creation speaks of the tenderness of God. Read some of these Scriptures concerning God's tenderness:

Isaiah 25:8: "The Sovereign Lord will wipe away the tears from all faces."

Revelation 21:4: "He will wipe every tear from their eyes. There will be no more death or mourning or crying or pain, for the old order of things has passed away."

Isaiah 46:3–4: "Listen to me, O house of Jacob, all you who remain of the house of Israel, you whom I have upheld since you were conceived, and carried since your birth. Even to your old age and gray hairs I am he, I am he who will sustain you."

The apostle Paul, when he wrote to the Thessalonian church, said, "We were gentle among you, like a mother caring for her little children. We loved you so much that we were delighted to share with you not only the gospel of God but our lives as well, because you had become so dear to us" (1 Thess. 2:7). In fact the phrase "fond affection" indicates the yearning love of a mother for her children.

Remember, Paul is a man's man. According to his own testimony in 2 Corinthians 11:24–28:

> Five times I received from the Jews the forth lashes minus one. Three times I was beaten with rods, once I was stoned, three times

I was shipwrecked, I spent a night and a day in the open sea, I have been constantly on the move. I have been in danger from rivers, in danger from bandits, in danger from my own countrymen, in danger from Gentiles; in danger in the city, in danger in the country, in danger at sea; and in danger from false brothers. I have labored and toiled and have often gone without sleep; I have known hunger and thirst and have often gone without food; I have been cold and naked. Besides everything else, I face daily the pressure of my concern for all the churches. Who is weak, and I do not feel weak? Who is led into sin, and I do not inwardly burn?

Did you notice what got to Paul most? Not the physical hardships so much as the emotional concerns and care for his people. Paul said earlier that he was "like a nursing mother." What are some of the characteristics of a nursing mother? Here are three key ones I have observed.

1. *The ability to be tender.* Have you ever noticed a mother nursing? I was recently in a mall and saw a mother carrying her little one with her. All of a sudden she stopped, sat on a bench, and prepared to feed her baby. She put down her packages, then gently placed her hand under the baby's head and ever so lovingly held the child up to her breast so the baby could get nourishment. A free man operates the same way. He assesses the needs of the moment and then acts accordingly. Tenderness requires empathy and a free man has the ability to show empathy. A free man, with the power of Christ within, is set free to not only feel his own feelings but also the feelings of others. He can stand by their side as Christ would and with tenderness wipe away their tears.

I received a package not too long ago that had these words written on the side of it: "Handle With Care; Contents Are Fragile." As I opened up the box I had received a coffee mug and some neat treats. If the contents had been thrown around the mug surely would have broken even though it was padded with newspapers. A free man recognizes that the relationships he has been given—with his family and friends—are to be handled with care because the contents are fragile.

A free man does not view himself in relationships as being above or below someone else—as being in a position of power or powerlessness. You know when you are with a free man because he doesn't talk at you, doesn't interrupt, and doesn't give advice without being asked. He listens and stands beside you, and in his presence you have an uncanny feeling you have been given permission to be yourself.

He lives with his wife in an understanding way and he doesn't provoke his children to anger. Walter Trobisch put it well when he said, "A redeemed motherly man holds his wife securely in his arms, even when he does know why she is crying. He spreads a blanket over her and sees that she is not cold. He stoops over to his child and takes him on his lap. The child is safe and can grow strong to meet the storms of life."[2]

But there is another key characteristic of being like a nursing mother.

2. *The ability to feel deeply.* A nursing mother has the ability to understand the grunts, groans, and gurgles of her child. When the baby cries, the mother also feels distress; when the baby is happy, she also feels pleasure; and if anyone were to try to harm her children, she would stand ready to protect the children—and not just when they are babies.

I have had grown men cry in my office over the choices and mistakes their children have made. These men cried because they knew a better way, but their children had to learn their lesson "the hard way." Jesus felt this way over Jerusalem when they would not accept him as their Savior. Luke 19:41 says, "As he approached Jerusalem and saw the city, he wept over it."

Jesus was also deeply upset when his friend, Lazarus, died: "When Jesus saw her [Mary] weeping, and the Jews who had come along with her weeping, he was deeply moved in spirit and troubled. . . . Jesus wept" (John 11:33, 35).

A free man can weep freely and express his emotions because he is now able to put himself in the place of others. He can truly "rejoice with those who rejoice and mourn with those who mourn" (Rom. 12:16).

A free man has learned that there is no pit so deep but what Jesus isn't deeper. He is not afraid to mourn and grieve his losses. In fact, he

knows that through his losses, God shows his strength. The apostle
Paul put it well when he said,

> [Jesus] said to me, "My grace is sufficient for you, for my
> power is made perfect in your weakness."
>
> Therefore I will boast all the more gladly about my weak-
> nesses, so that Christ's power may rest on me. That is why, for
> Christ's sake, I delight in weaknesses, in insults, in hardships, in
> persecutions, in difficulties. For when I am weak, then I am strong.
> (2 Cor. 12:9–10)

How a man deals with his losses shows his character and his faith
in God. Switching jobs, friends moving away, family problems, children beginning to leave the nest, losing his partner, a demotion at
work, and just change in itself can cause one to grieve. A man can feel
deeply because he has been to the ash heap and found God there
waiting for him. He has experienced the healing of God in the midst
of his hurt. "He who has been forgiven much . . . loves much." A free
man can feel deeply because he has tasted the goodness of God even
in his grief.

3. *A free man is able to touch and be touched.* A nursing mother
touches. She holds the child close to bring comfort as well as to show
approval and delight. There is something about being touched that
gives one a sense of affirmation, assurance, and acceptability.

I remember one man—six-foot-four, 210 pounds. He had blonde
hair and steel-blue eyes that could cut right through you. He was as
solid as a rock. He was also a Colorado state patrolman. I was invited
by the human resource department of the Colorado State Patrol to
come and do some training on posttraumatic stress syndrome. The
human resource department felt it would help the officers understand
the tremendous amount of stress they were under on a daily basis. They
also wanted me to give them strategies on how to deal with their stress.

I had a group of about seven or eight officers. The officer I
described earlier knew I was a counselor. He looked at me and said,
"Look, Rod, I am not a touchy or feely kind of guy. Okay?"

I said, "Don't worry—I will not touchy you or feely you."

We ended our session and I went home. About an hour later I received a call. An officer had been shot and killed. Apparently the officer had arrested some juveniles for stealing a car and one of the youths had a gun the officer did not see. As the officer put the boys in the back seat, one of them pulled out his gun and shot the officer.

I was called back to help debrief the officers on this shooting. In my group was the blue-eyed blonde rock. The dead officer was one of his best friends. I stood up in the middle of the group and said, "I want you to know how much I respect you and your grief at this time. All I can offer you is my understanding and a hug, if you want it. Sometimes a hug helps you to know that someone is there who cares. If any of you wants a hug—I am here."

What happened next blew me away. The officer who said he was not touchy or feely stood up, came towards me, and wrapped his big arms around me. I wrapped mine around him. And together . . . we cried . . . and cried . . . and cried. I was able to be Jesus in the flesh for him. He knew I was there for him, and through me, he also knew God was there for him as well. Even a tough Colorado state patrol- man needs to be touched. So do you and those around you.

Jesus touched. He held children close to him, washed the feet of the disciples, touched sick people, and even let them lay on his breast.

He allowed himself to be touched. He let a woman wash his feet with her tears and dry them with her hair (Luke 7:38), and he loved it when little children wanted to be with him. Touching someone is a tangible way of saying, "I am there for you—no matter what." Even Jesus, before he started his ministry, received the assurance and "touch" of his Father. In Matthew 3:17, when Jesus was being baptized by John, the Spirit of God "touched" Jesus by coming upon him. Then the Father said, "This is my Son, whom I love; with him I am well pleased." The Father in essence was saying, "Son, you have my full approval and the assurance I am with you."

A free man can touch others because he knows there is healing in a touch. Let me give you one more example.

Lee Shapiro is a retired judge. He also genuinely loves people. To show his love he began offering everybody a hug. His colleagues dubbed him the "hugging judge." The bumper sticker on his car reads, "Don't bug me! Hug me!"

About six years ago, Lee created what he calls his *Hugger Kit*. On the outside it reads "A heart for a hug." The inside contains thirty little red embroidered hearts with "stick'ems" on the back. Lee will take out his Hugger Kit, go around to people and offer them a little red heart in exchange for a hug. Lee has become so well known for this that he is often invited to keynote conferences and conventions, where he shares his message of unconditional love.

At a conference in San Francisco, the local news media challenged him by saying, "It's easy to give out hugs here in the conference to people who self-selected to be here. But this would never work in the real world." They challenged Lee to give away some hugs on the streets of San Francisco. Followed by a television crew from the local news station, Lee went out onto the street.

First he approached a woman walking by. "Hi, I'm Lee Shapiro, the hugging judge. I'm giving out these hearts in exchange for a hug."

"Sure," she replied.

"Too easy," challenged the local commentator.

Lee looked around. He saw a meter maid who was being given a hard time by the owner of a BMW to whom she was giving a ticket. Lee marched up to her, camera crew in tow, and said, "You look like you could use a hug. I'm the hugging judge, and I'm offering you one." She accepted.

The television commentator threw down one final challenge. "Look, here comes a bus. San Francisco bus drivers are the toughest, crabbiest, meanest people in the whole town. Let's see you get him to hug you." Lee took the challenge.

As the bus pulled up to the curb, Lee said, "Hi, I'm Lee Shapiro, the hugging judge. This has got to be one of the most stressful jobs in the whole wide world. I'm offering hugs to people today to lighten the load a little. Would you like one?" The six-foot-two, 230-pound bus driver got out of his seat, stepped down, and said, "Why not?"

Lee hugged him, gave him a heart, and waved good-bye as the bus pulled out. The TV crew was speechless. Finally, the commentator said, "I have to admit, I am very impressed."

One day Lee's friend Nancy Johnson showed up on his doorstep. Nancy said, "Grab a bunch of your Hugger Kits and let's go out to the home for the disabled."

When they arrived at the home, they started giving out balloon hats, hearts, and hugs to the patients. Lee was uncomfortable. He had never before hugged people who were terminally ill, severely retarded, or quadriplegic. It was definitely a stretch. But after a while it became easier, with Nancy and Lee acquiring an entourage of doctors, nurses, and orderlies who followed them from ward to ward.

After several hours they entered the last ward. These were thirty-four of the worst cases Lee had seen in his life. The feeling was so grim it took his heart away. But out of their commitment to share their love and to make a difference, Nancy and Lee started working their way around the room followed by the entourage of medical staff, all of whom by now had hearts on their collars and balloon hats on their heads.

Finally, Lee came to the last person, Leonard. Leonard was wearing a big white bib which he was drooling on. Lee looked at Leonard dribbling onto his bib and said, "Let's go, Nancy, there's no way we can get through to this person."

Nancy replied, "C'mon Lee. He's a fellow human being, isn't he?" Then she placed a funny balloon hat on Leonard's head. Lee took one of his little red hearts and placed it on Leonard's bib. He took a deep breath, leaned down and gave Leonard a hug.

All of a sudden Leonard began to squeal, "Eeeeeehh! Eeeeeehh!" Some of the other patients in the room began to clang things together.

Lee turned to find that every doctor, nurse, and orderly was crying. Lee asked the head nurse, "What is going on?"

Lee will never forget what she said: "This is the first time in twenty-three years we've ever seen Leonard smile."[3]

We are most like God—when we touch. Jesus did not come in a space suit so he would not be contaminated with our terminal illness called sin. No, he became flesh and dwelled among us—and touched us. A free man has received the healing touch of God and now freely gives that healing touch to those around him.

We have seen how a free man is free to show the tenderness of God, but he must also be able to balance that with the "tough love" of God. He also must be a fatherly man.

THE FATHERLY MAN

Walter Trobisch says that a fatherly man

is the strong, decisive, responsible, planning man who starts nurturing his wife so that she can become a good mother. He understands her in her cycle. His heart is filled with awe and wonder when he reflects that new life can come from an act of love. And that this new life is dependent on him, his protecting hand and loving care. He helps his wife in choosing a doctor who will not relieve him or rob him of his responsibility to coach his own baby's birth and will allow him to go to prenatal check-ups. He stays at his wife's side at the birth of their child. He provides a safe environment and strong encouragement during the nursing period, taking an active interest in the child's daily development and growth. He is wide awake, anticipating the pitfalls and dangers that his children may face. Because of that, they can place their confidence in him. On the other hand, if a child disappoints him, his world does not crumble. He does not receive his identity from his children, but from the Father from whom every family in heaven and on earth is named.

Such a father is the hero for his four-, five-, six-, seven-year-old child and older. When puberty comes, the child develops a strong desire toward independence, and even though he may find and seek outside heroes, the deep underlying knowledge is there: father is the best example to follow. By daring to take an active part in nurturing the whole family he has become the best example of a father. He has taught fatherliness to his sons and given his daughters the best guide for choosing a husband.[4]

Trobisch gives a clear description of the responsible and tough love side of a man ... the fatherly side. In fact, in Trobisch's description of the fatherly man there are three key ingredients to being fatherly.

The Fatherly Man Instructs

Deuteronomy 6:4–7 says,

> Hear, O Israel: The Lord our God, the Lord is one. Love the Lord you God with all your heart and with all your soul and with all your strength. These commandments that I give you today are to be upon your hearts. Impress them on your children. Talk about them when you sit at home and when you walk along the road, when you lie down and when you get up.

Notice two things in this verse. First, the emphasis is on the heart attitude of the one teaching. It is not merely instruction but the person's passion. These people are in love with God with all of their heart, soul, and body. Their love permeates all that they do. Talking about their God is as natural as breathing. There is no secular world and sacred world to them—just the world that all belongs to the Father—their Father.

Notice also that the teaching is directed toward sons. In the Hebrew culture the emphasis was on training up the next generation of leadership. The method of training was the father passing on his wisdom to his sons, who would be responsible for the nation's future. Also, it was assumed in the Hebrew culture that the father was the one doing the teaching. He was to be his son's mentor.

A fatherly man teaches his family. He loves his daughters and mentors his sons. He is the one who naturally shows his children the presence of God in their world.

We recently had a visit from my brother-in-law, Dave, his wife, Judy, and their three sons, Jeremy, the oldest, Nathan, the middle one, and Ben, the youngest. They had just taken a year-long adventure as a family. David, as a physical therapist, had the opportunity to take a leave of absence from his work and contract himself out to work at various clinics across the country. Since Judy homeschools the boys, this was no problem. So for the entire year they lived in Florida, Maryland, and many other states.

What amazed us, however, were the stories the children told me of how God had provided for them on their trip. For instance, their van had been stolen. This could have been a traumatic experience, but they were able to get a better van. The kids told me how God had met their needs in ways they couldn't fathom.

Even during their visit with us, David just naturally taught them about God. For instance, one evening they took a walk while the gorgeous Colorado sun set behind the mountains. It cast an orange glow. David said to his family, "Wow, isn't it neat that our God would provide such a great evening to our day?" The boys stood in awe and wonder and echoed the same sentiments as their dad.

A free man sees God in all that he does and then communicates those observations to his family. He is a man who teaches—because he himself is teachable.

A Fatherly Man Is Imitated

Research suggests that children learn moral behavior more from observing what others *do* than from what they *preach*. Children exposed to a hypocritical model—who does one thing and says another—tend to learn hypocrisy. It appears that young lives are formed not so much by the parent's intellectual beliefs as by habitual family practices.[5]

Consider these sayings:

Preach the gospel . . . and use words if necessary.

Walk your talk.

Practice what you preach.

All of these describe the fatherly man. He is a man of integrity.

About a year ago, the cover of the *New York Herald Tribune Sunday Magazine* displayed a picture of the Statue of Liberty, taken from a helicopter, showing the top of the statue's head. I was amazed at the detail. The sculptor had done a painstaking job with the lady's coiffure, and yet he must have been pretty sure that the only eyes that would ever see this detail would be the uncritical eyes of sea gulls. He could never have dreamed that anyone would fly over this head, but he was artist enough to finish off this part of the statue with as much care as he had devoted to her face, arms, torch, and everything else that people see as they sail by. What mattered to the artist was that the job was done right. Character is who you are when nobody is looking—and you never know who may be watching.

A fatherly man is consistent. Though not always perfect, he is authentic. What you see *is* what you get. He can say, "Follow me ... as I follow Christ."

A Fatherly Man Is Involved

I remember visiting a good friend of mine in Atlanta. He truly loves his family and creates an environment of care and involvement. He told me this story about his six-year-old daughter. He said they were getting ready to go on their father/daughter date when they could not find the keys to the car. His daughter, fearing that they would not be able to go on their date, started to cry.

Dad took her in his arms to comfort her. He said, "Let's ask Jesus to help us find the keys." His little girl folded her hands and prayed, "Jesus, I want to spend time with my daddy. Will you help us find the keys?"

After my friend prayed as well, he said to his little girl, "Now, you go that way and look on the couch, and I'll go this way and look in the kitchen."

After a few moments, he said he heard a shriek of excitement. He said his daughter came running to him with the keys in her hand. She shouted, "Jesus helped us find the keys!"

My friend picked up his excited little girl, and they thanked Jesus together for helping them find the keys.

My friend was involving his daughter in *his* love for Jesus so that she also might fall in love with Jesus as well. This dad was an *involved dad.*

A Fatherly Man Creates an Atmosphere for Growth

A good friend of mine was once offered a promotion—one that would mean greater prestige for him and more income for his family, and possibly a move to a new state. Furthermore, if he refused it, he might be passed over for future positions in the company. So he held a "family council" to seek the advice of his wife and children. At the time, his children were in their junior and senior years in high school, and his wife had a solid network of friends. Each family member expressed a desire to stay. After much prayer and thought, he decided not to take the position. Why?

He told me, "Rod, God has called me to create an environment where my family can grow and flourish. Just as you wouldn't take a healthy flower from the fertile soil it occupies, so also it would be foolish to take my family out of the fertile soil that is producing such quality and character in my kids and wife. Besides, I can always get another job—but I can't always have the environment I have for my family right now."

My friend developed what I call an open atmosphere in his home. His family felt comfortable and safe. There was spontaneity, feelings could be expressed, and fun could take place at any moment. They enjoyed each other, talked to each other, and shared their deepest feelings—no matter how hard. There were no untouchable areas and everyone's opinion was respected. Dad was the decision maker, but he welcomed input and took each person's concerns to heart. There was mutual trust and there was flexibility. My friend's family couldn't help but grow and flourish. A fatherly man operates from an open system.

And so did Jesus. There are no untouchable areas of discussion with Jesus. I can share my deepest pain and thoughts with him and know I will not be rejected. I know the Father wants to hear what I have to say and welcomes my input. A fatherly man creates this atmosphere because his Father has created it for him. He just passes it along.

A free man is both tender and tough—velvet and steel. No longer is he caught in the Child-Rearing Double Bind; the Feeling Double Bind; the Spontaneity Double Bind; the Companionship Double Bind, or the Gender Double Bind. By being both fatherly and motherly, he demonstrates that he is truly complete in Christ.

DISCUSSION QUESTIONS

1. In what ways has God shown his tenderness to you? Describe one.
2. Are you grieving any losses? If so—name them and then give them to the Lord.
3. Name two ways you will show God's tenderness to others this week.
4. As a fatherly man—name the characteristic that you feel is your greatest strength. What will you do to keep it strong? Which characteristic is your weakest? What will you do to strengthen it?

CHAPTER 10

The Peaceful Man

"If you're going to San Francisco," said a song of the sixties, "you're gonna meet some gentle people there." If you are steeped in the sixties culture, then you know about Jerry Garcia. He was, according to the *Washington Post*, "the rock oracle of the Grateful Dead, a band that epitomizes freedom." The *New York Times* said Garcia, a guitarist, was a "mellow icon of 60s idealism" and embodied "psychedelic optimism." The *Times* front-page obituary said that the Grateful Dead "symbolized a spirit of communal bliss."

You might think someone with the success of Jerry Garcia would be content. A man at peace. After all, his band was the most popular concert attraction anywhere, ever. When he died on August 9, 1995, as many Generation-Xers as gray-bearded boomers mourned.

Garcia had it all. Or so it seemed. He had money, influence, and fame. But like the generation he represented, things weren't all that blissful. Jerry Garcia was not a peaceful man. The freedom he epitomized didn't bring him peace. After the Dead's last concert in Chicago, Garcia checked into the Betty Ford Center in Rancho Mirage, California, to deal with the heroin habit he had been trying to overcome for years—that and his smoking and his eating. He had gotten married for the third time the year before.

Many men think that if they achieve financial success, they will be content. Others think a historic accomplishment will bring contentment. Yet men like Jerry Garcia stand as proof that such things don't bring contentment. A man's music may be bliss to decades of followers while the singer himself is filled with despair.

None of us wants to end up like Jerry Garcia. We don't want to search for contentment in things that won't satisfy. We've already seen that the double binds can cause psychological and emotional dissension. When we're in their clutches we feel like failures no matter what we do. If we devote ourselves to our families and slack off at work, we feel we have failed professionally. If we give ourselves to our work and devote less time to our families, our family suffers and we feel like failures as husbands and fathers. Each double bind carries with it a guarantee of discontentment.

But we have seen that escape is possible. We can take the steps necessary to find freedom. But does freedom itself guarantee contentment and peace? Not necessarily. Freedom is, however, the doorway through which we can find peace. In this chapter, I want to explore how a free man can become a peaceful man.

A PEACEFUL MAN LIVES WITH AMBIGUITIES

One day a woman was riding into town with a friend when she noticed a radar detector mounted on the dashboard of her friend's car. "Sally," she asked, "why do you have a Fuzzbuster?"

"For my birthday, I asked my husband for a Dustbuster," she replied. "This is what I got."

It's easy to see how Sally's husband misunderstood her. Dustbuster and Fuzzbuster do sound alike. But the story illustrates how men often hear only what they want to hear. In the spiritual realm we do the same thing. When Jesus promised his followers peace, it would be easy to assume that this means we will have a life free of difficulty. After all, that is what we want. I know it's what I want.

Conflicting Desires

But this isn't the case. The peace Jesus promised enables us to live with the ambiguities of life. It helps us find stability when the world around us is shaking. That is what Jesus experienced, and it's what he offers us.

On the night of his betrayal, Jesus struggled with the tension between his desire to avoid the cross, and his desire to obey his Father. Jesus found himself in the viselike grip of two competing desires. So intense was his struggle that he sweat drops like blood (Luke 22:39–46). He was in a double bind. If he went with his feelings he would avoid the cross and disobey his Father. If he submitted to his Father, Jesus would have to endure the cross. In the midst of that situation he found the right path and took it. I don't think the Lord's decision to drink the cup, which contained all the suffering of the cross, meant his desire to avoid the pain went away. He moved forward and took the ambiguity with him.

Jesus then left Gethsemane and walked to the cross with no expression of anxiety. In fact, Jesus demonstrated greater calm than anyone else during the ordeal of his trials and crucifixion. Think about it: Judas betrayed him; his disciples panicked and ran away; Peter denied knowing him; the religious leaders mocked and beat him.

In the midst of his contradictory feelings and all that turbulence, Jesus found peace. And so can you. But it won't come if you believe you have to get rid of all of the ambiguities of life. Conflicting desires, dreams, pressures, and feelings are a part of life. Peace isn't getting rid of all such conflicts but learning to live with them.

What I Am vs. What I Want to Be

Awhile back I was having a great round of golf. At least on the front-nine. Everything I hit went just where I wanted it to go. I was realizing my potential. Then I came to the tenth hole. I placed my ball on the tee, gripped my club, and took a few practice swings. I was at peace with myself, God, and the world around me. Everything was in harmony.

Finally, I swung my driver up and brought it down with speed and power. Not to mention a touch of class. I hit the ball and felt that sweet moment when the ball explodes off the tee and rockets across the blue sky. Only this time something was wrong. The ball sliced so sharply I wondered if it was a boomerang. Without a thought I slammed the club down with force on the ground and shouted my disdain. Even if I could find the ball in the brush, I wasn't sure what I would do with it. Not that it would matter, the hole would be a disaster.

My frustrations on the golf course often occur because of the difference between what I want to be and what I am. It's a conflict between those times when my game is sharp and those occasions when it stinks. The more I am able to live with that ambiguity, the more I enjoy the game.

The same is true in the Christian life. As followers of Christ we look at Jesus and see how we are supposed to think and act. Sometimes we are on target. At other times we are as off course as a sliced golf ball. Finding peace occurs when we realize that the Christian life, like golf, is a process.

The apostle Paul said, "In Him all the fullness of Deity dwells in bodily form, and in Him you have been made complete" (Colossians 2:10, NASB). But even though Paul said we have been made complete in Christ, that doesn't mean we're finished. The apostle also told the Philippians, "Not that I have already obtained it [the resurrection from the dead], or have already become perfect, but I press on in order that I may lay hold of that for which also I was laid hold of by Christ Jesus" (Phil. 2:12, NASB).

Paul had peace with the tension that exists between the process and the product. He knew that he hadn't spiritually arrived. The apostle realized he wasn't everything he would one day be. He found peace in the midst of the fact that he was still in process as a follower of Christ. And so must we. Like a golfer, we should aim for par but realize we may not reach it every time. Peace is experienced when we realize we are a project, and so is every other man.

A PEACEFUL MAN IS SHELTERED

When caught in a double bind, a man experiences extreme frustration. No matter what he does, he loses. Once free, however, there are still ambiguities that a man must learn to live with.

One reason a man can do this is because he has found shelter—he's been accepted by his heavenly Father and has a spiritual roof over his head. He knows the location of his home.

Walter Trobisch observed that when God created Adam, he had already created a home for him.[1] A place of his own. Eden was an ideal setting, but when Adam sinned not only was he separated from God, but he was removed from his home—his place in the world. Since the Fall, all men long for a place of their own, a place where they belong, a home. Without it, there is no peace, only a continual sense of restlessness.

As followers of Christ we have found our home, but it isn't a place. It's a Person. David said, "You prepare a table before me in the presence of my enemies" (Psalm 23:5). Later he wrote, "From the ends of the earth I call to you, I call as my heart grows faint; lead me to the rock that is higher than I. For you have been my refuge, a strong tower against the foe" (Psalm 61:2–3).

In my travels I have seen some of the most beautiful spots in the world, and each time I gaze at a natural wonder, I can't help but marvel at the genius of God to have created such beauty. Yet the old saying is true: "There's no place like home." Even on long trips, like my recent one to Australia, I can't wait to get back home. Nothing feels as good as driving into my driveway, walking in the front door of my house, and being greeted by my wife, Nancy.

All of us long to be home. We know the comfort of getting there. But the home God gives us is always with us. It's not a place we travel to, but a Person who is beside us. Those who know God are sheltered by him. I've seen that such men realize some crucial truths about God.

God Is Powerful Enough to Protect Us

In Ohio we have some pretty harsh winters. Occasionally, the wind howls over the open fields. As a boy, I would sometimes get scared, but my father was always there to calm my fears. Growing up in the shadow of such a powerful man, I learned what it means to feel safe in his shelter. While he couldn't calm the winds, he did protect me. If my earthly father, with his limited power, could give me such peace, how much more can our all-powerful God impart peace to his children? The psalmist understood this.

> God is our refuge and strength,
>   an ever-present help in trouble.
> Therefore we will not fear, though the earth give way
>   and the mountains fall into the heart of the sea,
> though its waters roar and foam
>   and the mountains quake with their surging.
> There is a river whose streams make glad the city of God,
>   the holy place where the Most High dwells.
> God is within her, she will not fall;
>   God will help her at break of day.
> Nations are in uproar, kingdoms fall;
>   he lifts his voice, the earth melts.
> The Lord Almighty is with us;
>   the God of Jacob is our fortress.
> (Psalm 46:1–7)

The terrifying dangers the psalmist spoke about were both physical and political. He imagined an earthquake so devastating that it shook mountains and stirred oceans. In the face of such natural disasters, there would be no place to hide, no house would stand, no ship would stay afloat.

1. *God protects us from physical danger.* Maybe you have stared physical danger in the face. If so, then you may know the terrifying power of an earthquake, forest fire, tornado, or other natural disaster. I do. I lived in Houston, Texas, when a hurricane hit that gulf-coast city. Everybody was warned about the danger. We were urged to evacuate. But Nancy and I decided to sit out the storm. How bad could it be?

I will never forget the howling winds. Never have I seen such power. But then an amazing thing happened. After several hours there was perfect calm. Nancy and I went outside and discovered that the wind had completely died down. When we looked up we could see blue sky. Amazingly, the eye of the hurricane had passed directly over us. All around us, in every direction, were hurricane force winds that were tearing up Houston and its suburbs, but we were in a place of perfect peace.

God offers us that. No matter what dangers we might encounter, when we run to God, we find ourselves in the eye of the storm. We have One who gives shelter regardless of what is happening.

Of course, that doesn't mean we will never be hurt. Nor does it mean danger won't overcome us. But we can be sure that every hardship and every physical danger we face must pass through the hands of our God. It is designed for our good (Romans 8:28).

2. *God protects us from political dangers.* Many believe that the scene described in Psalm 46 is the same event spoken of by the prophet Isaiah (Isaiah 36–37). At that time the Egyptians and Assyrians were the two greatest nations on earth. In 705 B.C. Sennacherib became the king of Assyria. Before he assumed the throne, however, the empire had begun to crumble and many of the kings under its rule had rebelled. In the first three years of his reign, Sennacherib tried to consolidate his strength. He moved south into Babylonia and brought those kings under his dominion once more. But the kings to the west, toward Egypt, continued to rebel. One of those kings was Hezekiah of Judah.

Seeking to restore his kingdom to its former glory, Sennacherib knew he had to battle Egypt for world dominion. He moved down a highway between Assyria to the north and east, and Egypt to the south and west. And Israel was caught in a nutcracker squeeze. In 701 B.C. Sennacherib moved down through Palestine like a raging flood. His generals were military geniuses, and he was a half-mad conqueror. His armies swept through the cities of Phoenicia, which fell before him like twigs in a raging river. He turned to the cities of Judah and one by one they crumbled until he came to the capital city of Jerusalem. At that moment Hezekiah, the king of Judah, knew he was in trouble.

He tried to bribe the conquering king, but Sennacherib simply took the bribe and continued his approach. Finally, the Assyrian ruler stood before the city of God, and, in his own words, he had Hezekiah shut up like a bird in a cage.

In that dark moment God told Hezekiah not to worry. God let the ruler of Judah know that while Sennacherib may have boxed in the king of Judah, he hadn't boxed in Judah's God.

It was suddenly no-contest. Sennacherib had no more of a chance against God than a little-league football team would have against the Dallas Cowboys. It was like a bantam weight amateur boxer taking on Mike Tyson.

One night as the Jewish people went to bed, an army of almost 200,000 men sat outside their walls. Except for God's promise, the people of Jerusalem seemed doomed.

Have you ever faced a situation in which you felt destined for defeat? Have the odds ever seemed stacked against you? Hezekiah must have felt that same way. But the next morning when the people awoke, 186,000 Assyrian soldiers lay dead in the fields outside Jerusalem. And what of Sennacherib? He took off like a dog with its tail between its legs.

No wonder the psalmist said the "God of angel armies protects us" (Psalm 46:7).

3. *God is all-powerful.* The next time you are overwhelmed by a problem, consider these facts: the nearest star to the earth is Alpha Centauri, four-and-a-half light years away. That means its light, traveling at 186,000 miles a second, takes four-and-a-half years to reach the earth. And that's the *nearest* star. Flung out into space where naked eye has never seen and where telescope has seldom seen are stars whose light is just now coming into vision, even though they were created at the dawn of time.

Or look at it another way. The earth is 93 million miles from the sun. Its surface is 11,890 times greater than that of the earth. The sun has a volume that is 1,300,000 times that of the earth. That means if you took an earth and dropped it into the sun every second it would take more than fifteen days to fill it.

The largest star we know about is the star Alpha Hercules. It is so large that 512 million of our suns could be put into it. It would hold 670 million million earths. If we could drop one earth into Alpha Hercules every second, it would take 21,100,000 years to fill it.

Contemplate the magnitude of the stars that fill the universe and the immense distances between them. Then consider the words of the psalmist: "He stretches out the heavens like a tent" (Psalm 104:2). Our God is so great that he grabbed the corners of the universe like a pup-tent and spread it out before him. Amazing! The next time you face an intimidating problem, glance at your problem and then gaze at the God who shelters you. No matter how great your difficulty, God can handle it.

It is possible that as you consider the power of God you may think, "What sort of a God is this? He's certainly powerful, but does he really care about me? Will he use his power for someone like me?" The psalmist answered this question when he said that "the God of Jacob is our fortress" (Psalm 46:7).

4. *God is personal.* To appreciate those words—a "Jacob-wrestling God fights for us"—you need to remember who Jacob was. He was the man who tricked his brother and then stole his inheritance. Years later, after God had humbled Jacob, the two wrestled. Jacob begged for a blessing and God gave it to him.

If God would bless a man like Jacob, he will also bless you. The One who shelters you not only has the power to protect you, he has the desire to do so.

Please don't misunderstand me. As I mentioned before, this doesn't mean we win every battle. Finding shelter in God doesn't mean life will be easier. But it does mean we can have peace in the midst of our problems.

Hebrews 11 names the great men and women of faith whose stories are found in the Old Testament, people who trusted in God and experienced great victories. But the chapter ends by recognizing those who trusted in God and endured hardship, some even suffering death. But in the midst of life's greatest dangers, they remained under God's shelter. And they found peace.

On December 17, 1850, Captain Allen Gardiner and six companions landed at Patagonia on the southern tip of South America. They had made that long journey to bring the gospel to a people so primitive that evolutionist Charles Darwin said they existed "in a

lower state . . . than in any other part of the world." Gardiner had prepared himself and his crew for the mission. He had made two previous visits to the region and knew that the natives were ruthless canni-
bals and that the land and weather were treacherous. His team
included a doctor and a carpenter, and they brought with them a half
years supply of food and other goods. Gardiner's supporters in England had committed to send a relief ship of food after six months.

After his departure from England, Gardiner wrote, "Nothing can
exceed the cheerful endurance and unanimity of the whole party. . . . I
feel that the Lord is with us, and cannot doubt that He will own and
bless the work which He has permitted us to begin."

But something went wrong. The month after his departure, Gardiner's supporters could not find a ship to carry the next six-months
provisions to Patagonia. No one wanted to make such a dangerous
journey. So as the missionaries carried out their work on the cold tip
of South America and as their supplies ran low, they scanned the hori-
zon for the approaching ship. It never arrived. Those men faced a
tough test. Alone in a hostile environment, without food or other supplies, hunger and death haunted them.

By the time a relief ship finally reached Patagonia in October of
1851, the missionaries had all died of starvation. Clad in three suits,
with wool stockings over his arms to ward off the numbing cold, Gardiner's emaciated body was found lying beside a boat.

What had that English missionary thought about during those
last horrifying days? Had the trial destroyed his faith? Were his dying
days filled with nothing but pain? At one point, Gardiner wrote: "Poor
and weak as we are, our boat is very Bethel to our soul, for we feel
and know that God is here. Asleep or awake, I am, beyond the power
of expression, happy."[2]

Imagine. In the face of certain death, Captain Allen Gardiner
found shelter in God. And within that shelter he found not simply
peace, but happiness.

Down But Not Out

The apostle Paul understood this. In the face of life's ambiguities and hardships, he too found that God would shelter him, and that prompted him to say, "We are hard pressed on every side, but not crushed; perplexed, but not in despair; persecuted, but not abandoned; struck down, but not destroyed" (2 Corinthians 4:8–9).

Several years ago, a six-year-old nephew ran up to me and said, "I want to show you how strong I am." He then led me into his bedroom where he had a plastic punching bag. It stood three feet high and looked like a clown. Every time he hit it, the clown fell back and then popped right back up.

"I'll get it down," I told him. "Move over and watch this."

I then hit the clown in the mouth with all of my strength. It fell back and then popped back up again. No matter how hard or how frequently I hit the clown, it came back up.

When I examined it I learned why. It was weighted on the bottom with sand. When a man knows who he is—and whose he is—he may be knocked down, but he always gets back up. He is balanced by his identify in God. He may be down, but he's never out.

Discussion Questions

1. What kind of tension is produced when we compare what we are with what we want to be? What is the source of this tension? How is it resolved?
2. Since we will never be free of every ambiguity in life, how do we find peace?
3. God has the power to protect us from all danger! Identify the threats you're presently facing and identify how God can protect you. What must you do to experience his protection?
4. What are some of the things you've done that makes you *feel* like God might not want a relationship with you? How does the story of Jacob offer hope to every person who has sinned against God? How does it offer you hope?

5. Reread the story about Allen Gardiner out loud. As you read
    ask God for the strength you need to respond to disappoint-
    ment with the kind of peaceful attitude Allen Gardiner had.

CHAPTER 11

The Authentic Man

Chances are you've never heard the name Erich Weiss. I know I hadn't. Yet by the time of his death, he was world-famous. Weiss was born of Hungarian-Jewish parents in Appleton, Wisconsin, in 1874. He became the highest-paid entertainer of his day. In his time, Weiss was as well-known an entertainer as Demi Moore and Tom Hanks are today.

He was a master showman, a distinguished flyer, a mystifying magician, and most of all—an unsurpassed "escapologist." His stage name? Harry Houdini. No doubt that is a name you recognize.

On March 10, 1904, London's *Daily Illustrated Mirror* challenged Houdini to escape from a special pair of handcuffs they had prepared. Are you ready? There were six locks on each cuff and nine tumblers on each lock. Seven days later, four thousand spectators gathered in the London Hippodrome to witness the outcome of the audacious challenge that Houdini had accepted.

At precisely 3:15 P.M., the manacled showman stepped into an empty cabinet that came up to his waist. He knelt down and remained out of sight for twenty minutes. He stood up smiling as the crowd applauded, thinking he was free. But he was not. He asked for more light. As they came on even brighter, he knelt out of sight again. Fifteen minutes later he stood up. Applause broke out—again, premature. He was still handcuffed. He said he needed to flex his knees.

Down into the cabinet went the magician again. Twenty minutes passed slowly for the murmuring crowd before Houdini stood to his feet with a broad smile. The loud applause quickly stopped when the audience saw that he was still not free. Because the bright lights made the heat so intense, he leaped from the cabinet and twisted the manacled hands in front of him until he could reach a pocket knife in his vest. Opening the knife with his teeth, he held its handle in his mouth and bent forward to such a degree that the tail of his coat fell over his head. He grasped the coat, pulled it over his head, then proceeded to slash it to ribbons with the knife between his teeth. Throwing aside the strips of his heavy coat, he jumped back into the box as the audience roared its approval and cheered him on.

Down went Houdini, but this time for only ten minutes. With a dramatic flourish, he jumped from the box—wrists free—waving the bulky handcuffs over his head in triumph. Pandemonium exploded in London. Once again the showman had achieved the incredible—almost the impossible.

Afterward, with a twinkle in his eyes, Houdini told reporters that his ability to escape was based on "knowledge."[1]

Perhaps as we have looked at the double binds that trap men, you feel as though handcuffs have been placed on your wrists and each cuff has six locks with nine tumblers. Unlike Houdini, you don't know how to get free. You struggle, but escape eludes you. To make matters worse, you feel others—your wife, children, friends, and coworkers—are watching you struggle. No matter how hard you try, you can't break free of the Autonomy Double Bind, the Hero Image Double Bind, the Feeling Double Bind, and every other bind.

I know how you feel. I've been there. And I've worked with countless other men who struggled to get free of their double binds. The good news is the same thing that Houdini used to get free is there for you. I'm talking about knowledge. Experiencing freedom begins with knowing what freedom looks like and then discovering how to achieve it.

A free man is an authentic man. *Webster's Dictionary* defines *authentic* as that which is fully trustworthy because it is aligned with reality. An authentic man's view of himself and the world around him is consistent with reality. It's accurate. An authentic man is a "real" man. He's the genuine article.

I like these two definitions because they have special meaning for the follower of Christ. On the one hand, we want to be connected with reality. We want our perception of ourselves and the world around us to be accurate. And we also want our lives to conform to the life of Christ. We want to be authentic representatives of him.

This means we need two things. First, we need to understand what an authentic man looks like. And second, we need to see authenticity demonstrated by Jesus so we can follow his example.

THE DRIVING RANGE

By now you've guessed that I have a passion for golf. Because I travel so much, I take my clubs with me on the road. If I can't make it to a course, then I like to stop at a driving range. It is especially helpful to practice at a range that has flagged pins posted at various distances. While it feels good to hit a ball 300 yards no matter where it lands, it improves my game more to target particular flags at various distances. If I can place the ball close to a pin on the driving range, then I'm more likely to hit the ball accurately on the golf course.

Most men are like that with life. They find it helps to know where they're supposed to be headed. In counseling sessions I try to help men connect with their inner reality and then work on identifying the traits in Christ they want to copy. With that in mind, let's examine five emotional characteristics of an authentic man.

The Authentic Man's Emotions Are Immediate

An authentic man is connected to his feelings. He may not know what his emotions mean, but at least he experiences them consciously.

A man caught in the double binds has learned to ignore his emotions. We saw, for instance, that in the Gender Bind, a man is afraid to stay in touch with any of his feminine traits because he doesn't want to be seen as wimpy by his friends. By suppressing these feelings he becomes alienated from an important part of himself. He may at times feel like crying, but won't let himself. If he even *feels* like crying he may think of himself as less of a man. After all, real men don't cry!

Often, a man's conscious thoughts are disconnected from his emotions. And he can't seem to get them together. On the other hand, an authentic man is immediately conscious of his feelings because he knows who he is. He understands that his feminine feelings are part of being a man. When those emotions well up, he isn't afraid of them. He's in touch with them.

In Gethsemane Jesus not only felt extreme grief, he expressed it to his disciples. He told them he was so depressed, that he was on the verge of death (Matt. 26:38). To understand why Jesus was in touch with his feelings we only need to go back a few hours in the story. Earlier in the night, while in the upper room, the words of John make it clear Jesus knew exactly who he was (John 13:3). He understood his relationship with his Father and his destiny. Jesus wasn't searching for an identity. *He knew!* That knowledge gave him the ability to connect with all of his emotions—even the negative ones.

The Authentic Man Is Spontaneous

He responds quickly to what he's feeling and to what's happening around him. A man trapped in the Spontaneity Double Bind can't do that. He may feel like letting go at times, he may want to express himself and have a little fun, but he fears that if he does so, he'll make those around him uncomfortable. So what does he do? He stuffs his feelings. He disconnects from those feelings of spontaneity.

Since men always view other men as competitors, they don't want to appear foolish, lest they give an edge to the competition. I am reminded of the story of a man who stopped at a country store while driving through the south. While paying for a soft drink, the man noticed a group of men playing cards with a Great Dane.

"Can that dog really play cards?" the tourist asked.

"You bet."

"That's incredible!" the man exclaimed.

"Not really," said the clerk.

"You're kidding," said the visitor.

"Naw, he ain't as bright as all that. Whenever he gets a good hand, he wags his tail."

We're afraid if we act spontaneously, we'll give away our winnings. And we don't want to do that. But Jesus certainly acted spontaneously. While traveling through Samaria he stopped at a well and spoke with a Samaritan woman (John 4:7–38). While walking into Jericho he had lunch with a tax collector (Luke 19:1–10). There's no indication in the text that either of these meetings was planned. Spontaneous acts like these got Jesus into trouble with the religious leaders. Why? Because he didn't fit into their mold of what a religious leader should do.

It's refreshing to meet someone who, like Jesus, is spontaneous. A friend of mine related a liberating experience he once had. As payment for speaking at a conference, he was allowed to stay in the guest quarters of a wealthy business tycoon's estate on one of the San Juan Islands.

"After showing me around his estate," my friend said, "he took me for a ride in an antique car. The guy was crazy. He joked around with sales clerks in stores. He teased the attendant who put gas in his car. But he wasn't always playful. He could get serious too."

My friend said he used to be spontaneous like that when he was younger. But as a man he didn't want to be viewed as immature, so he settled down. Seeing a respected Christian businessman act with such freedom took the cuffs off his own spirit.

I suspect if you and I could spend an afternoon with Jesus, the same thing would happen to us.

The Authentic Man Knows What's Going on Inside

It would be easy to assume that an authentic man experiences emotions and then spontaneously does whatever he feels like doing. That is not the case. Instead, an authentic man identifies what is happening inside himself. He feels and then he processes what he's feeling.

He activates his mental X-ray machine so he can see what's happening inside. If something is broken, he finds out. If there is pain, but nothing is fractured, he makes note of that. If everything is okay, he recognizes that.

The thought occurred to me that one reason Jesus spent so much time in prayer may have been to discover what was happening within himself. He may have been praying so he could process his human emotions with the help of his heavenly Father.

While studying for my Ph.D. I had to participate in an on-going therapy group. Initially, the experience was intriguing. But as my defense mechanisms began to erode, I learned self-discovery wasn't always pleasant. I found things about myself I didn't like, things I had hidden from myself and others. But then something wonderful happened. I learned how to get in touch with my feelings and fears. I discovered I could accept myself. I began the lifelong process of identifying what is going on within—a process authentic men embrace.

The Authentic Man Gets His Feelings Out

But there is another step that needs to be taken. After we've identified what's happening inside, we need to express it. We need to get it all out. Sometimes that's not so easy. In fact, it can be downright painful.

We have all had a splinter in our hands. If it's a big one, with the tip sticking through the surface of our skin, we can grab the splinter with a pair of tweezers and pull it out. But if the splinter breaks off and a portion remains in our hand, that sliver of wood can cause a painful little infection that won't get better until all of the splinter is removed. I don't know about you, but I don't like digging into my hand with a needle. I've done it plenty of times. I suspect you have too.

On a more serious level, when doctors diagnose a patient with cancer, they know they must get *all* of the cancer out or the disease will spread. Negative emotions can be like a splinter or like cancer. They can be trivial or serious, but in either case, they need to be gotten out.

They need to be expressed. While the process may be painful, the result is always good. Expressing negative emotions produces emotional health.

Jesus certainly knew that. As he entered the Garden of Gethsemane he took Peter, James, and John with him. The other disciples remained at the gate. Once in the garden, Jesus separated himself a short distance from his three friends and fell to the ground to pray. What did he say? He expressed his desire to avoid the agony of the cross. Yet he indicated his willingness to obey his Father (Matt. 26:36–46).

That is *what* Jesus said. But *how* did he say it? In Hebrews 5:7 we read, "During the days of Jesus' life on earth, he offered up prayers and petitions with loud cries and tears to the one who could save him from death, and he was heard because of his reverent submission."

The disciples, who were sleeping only a stone's throw away, would have learned a lot if they could have heard Jesus express his negative feelings to God. They would have heard the Lord weeping loudly. Jesus literally got it all out. He expressed his feelings to God and then subordinated himself to the purpose of God. After expressing his pain, the Lord left the garden and walked courageously to the cross. Getting our pain out in the open enables us to unload any excess baggage so we can move forward with our lives.

The Authentic Man's Expressions of Emotion Are Appropriate

Now don't misunderstand me. I'm not suggesting we vent our emotions without thought. On the contrary, an authentic man doesn't fly off the handle when he's frustrated or angry. He processes his feelings before he expresses them. An authentic man recognizes his need to think through his feelings and then connect with others, then he operates consciously and acts appropriately.

I have observed that the greater a man's emotional outburst the more likely it is that he hasn't processed his thoughts and feelings before expressing them. We want to be men who don't let the emotional garbage pile up. We need to keep the emotional slate clean.

One modern convenience I especially appreciate is the ATM (automatic teller machine). I can stick my card into the slot, punch in my identification number, and presto—I get my money. I'm also thankful for my savings account, into which I can put away money, let it grow, and from which I can spend it later.

Unfortunately, in the area of emotions, men often use their savings account more than their ATM machine. It is characteristic of men to suffer a hurt, feel angry, and stuff their feelings. Weeks or months later that anger has grown, and when it's expressed it is much more destructive.

We need to avoid stashing away our feelings so we can spend them later. The moment we feel something, we need to get in touch with it, process it, and express it in an appropriate way. And an appropriate expression of our emotions is one that benefits the recipient. Our desire should be to minister to others through our words.

At times Jesus' words were gentle and comforting, as when he talked with the woman caught in adultery (John 8:1–11). On other occasions they were hard and confrontive, as when he rebuked Peter (Matt. 16:21–23). In every situation, Jesus was in touch with his emotions and expressed them appropriately.

HOW TO GET THERE

I have described five characteristics of an authentic man. But the question remains: how can we become such men? Here are two steps and a word of caution that I think are essential.

Step One: Cultivate Your Relationship with God

It is only natural for us to look to other people to meet our deepest emotional needs. The problem is, they can't! Asking them to do so is like drawing water from a dry well. People aren't equipped to fill our emotional cup—only God can do that.

Dr. Larry Crabb notes two reasons why we should depend on God to meet our needs. First, he gives us security. He loves us with a love we never deserved. He sees everything ugly in us and still loves us. In his love we find security.

Second, he gives us significance. The Holy Spirit has graciously and sovereignly equipped every believer to participate in God's great purpose of bringing all things together in Christ.[2] God has a wonderful plan for your life—and that makes you an important person!

Our problem is we are often so driven to succeed in the here and now that we fail to see what God has in store for us. Have you ever seen a *Magic Eye Card*? They are amazing to look at. They are cards with hidden 3-D images. The only way you can see the hidden picture is by placing the card right in front of your eyes and staring at it for several minutes. If you look long enough the image will suddenly come into view.

In a sense, that's what we need to do with the Bible. We need to look into it long enough that its pictures come into view. While a quick glance at its message sometimes helps us, it doesn't give us a clear picture. We need to look long and hard at the Bible. As we do so, we'll realize some amazing things about ourselves. Consider:

- You are a child of the Creator, the Ruler of the universe (John 1:12).
- You are a joint heir with Jesus Christ—all he has is yours (Romans 8:17).
- God the Father loves you as much as he loves Jesus (John 17:23).
- You are seated with Christ in the heavenlies (Colossians 3:1–3).
- Christ literally lives in you (Galatians 2:20).

These are only a few of the wonderful truths that are yours. Cultivating your relationship with God involves spending time in his Word so you can see who your are and what you have in him.

Cultivating a relationship with God also involves talking with him. Because I travel a lot it would be easy for my wife, Nancy, and I to drift apart. We overcome that tendency by talking on the phone. I hate to think how distant we would feel if we didn't see each other or talk for a couple of weeks.

Because God is a person, deepening your relationship with him involves talking. You can shoot up little prayers throughout the day, but you can also set aside some quiet time every day for prayer. If you're like me, that may be hard because you are busy. And you may wonder what you should say when you pray.

I encourage men to schedule a time slot they know they can manage. It is better to pray for five minutes every day than plan on praying for thirty minutes and never do it.

Keeping a prayer journal helps me focus when I pray. Otherwise, in the middle of a prayer I will catch myself trying to solve the world monetary problem, negotiating for peace in the Middle East, or figuring out how Ohio State can win its next game. Writing down my prayers helps me concentrate.

When I mention a prayer journal I'm not talking about anything fancy. A spiral notebook will do. And the prayers I write aren't pieces of literature. Nobody else will ever see them. I just jot down my feelings and thoughts. I pray specifically for my family and friends. I date my prayers and when they're answered I record that.

Whether writing my prayers in a journal or speaking them aloud, I always try to be honest with God. The psalms are filled with expressions of grief, frustration, fear, disappointment, and anger. You can open the book of Psalms almost anywhere and find deep expressions of emotion. But after pouring out their heart honestly to God, the psalmists always found comfort and joy.

You too need to be able to express your feelings honestly to God. If you can't do that then you won't be honest with other men. As you cultivate your prayer life, determine to be totally open. And remember, getting to know God is like running or lifting weights, consistency is crucial. A little bit every day will go a long way toward making you an authentic man! But there is another step we need to take.

Step Two: Cultivate Your Relationship with Men

Sometimes it shocks men when I tell them that they need more than God. That almost sounds sacrilegious. But it isn't. After creating Adam, didn't God say that it wasn't good for the man to be alone

(Genesis 2:18)? Adam lived in an ideal environment. He was without sin and had unbroken fellowship with God. Yet Adam needed another person. And so do you and I. We were created for relationship. And if we want to be authentic men, we must cultivate relationships with other men. While I addressed this subject earlier, I want to share a few additional thoughts.

A famous psychiatrist was leading a symposium on methods of getting patients to open up during a counseling session. The psychiatrist challenged his colleagues with a blatant boast: "I'll wager that my technique will enable me to get a new patient to talk about the most private things during the first session without my having to ask a question." What was his magic formula? Simply this. He began the session by revealing to the patient something personal about himself—a secret with which the patient might damage the doctor by breaking the confidence. However questionable we may regard the doctor's manipulation, it had the desired effect: it released the patient to talk.[3]

This principle applies to all human relationships. If you want to draw close to other men you need to be vulnerable. If you will take the first step of self-revelation, other men are more likely to open up with you. Your openness will create a safe place for them to talk about their greatest fears. They'll see you as less of a competitor and more of a friend.

Time and again Jesus was transparent with his disciples. He ate with them, slept under the stars with them, prayed with them, cried with them, resolved their arguments. He opened up with them and explained exactly who he was. When they didn't understand, he grieved. But he never closed them out. He told them, "I have called you friends, for everything that I learned from my Father I have made known to you" (John 15:15).

Don't misunderstand. I'm not advocating that you let it all hang out the first time you meet with another man or with a small group of men. Rather, slowly peel away the layers of your life and allow them to see who you are. As you do, they will probably become open with you as well. In time, you will feel safe in sharing your innermost thoughts, feelings, and fears.

A Word of Caution: You Will Be Let Down

It's important to know that your friends will probably let you down some time or another. Only God will never disappoint you. Ultimately, you must let him fill your emotional and spiritual cup. When a close friend disappoints or hurts you, you need to be willing to forgive.

One of the more touching stories in the Bible is powerful because of what is *not* said. The night before his crucifixion, Jesus told Peter that the disciple would deny him three times. Peter boldly declared that he would die before such a thing would happen. Jesus assured Peter that before the rooster crowed twice, Peter would deny him three times (Matt. 26:34). Of course, Peter did deny knowing Jesus, and afterward, he wept bitterly (Matt. 26:75).

It's not hard to imagine how Peter must have felt. He denied knowing the One he loved the most. He violated his own sense of right and wrong. Three days later he entered an empty tomb and realized Jesus had been raised from the dead. What would that mean for Peter? Utter joy, of course. But also, perhaps, failure, uselessness, shame at his own actions. Peter must have feared all of these and more.

Then the risen Jesus met with Peter—in private (Luke 24:34). As far as we know from Scripture, Peter is the only disciple whom the risen Lord met alone. Peter may have been sitting in a room grieving about what he had done, and he probably feared seeing Jesus. But as Peter was caught up in his thoughts, the Lord appeared before him.

What happened? We can't know for sure. That's the part of the story that isn't recorded. But we can guess. I think Jesus wrapped his strong arms around the crying fisherman and said, "It's okay Peter. I forgive you."

There have been times I needed forgiveness, and Jesus never withheld it. Not for a minute. And brother, that's exactly what you and I need to do when our friends let us down. Instead of being surprised by their shortcomings, we need to accept and forgive them.

Authentic men can do that because they know God has forgiven them. Since their emotional bank is filled with forgiveness, they can write forgiveness checks and give them to a friend.

CULTIVATE ENTHUSIASM

I opened the chapter with a story about Harry Houdini. Before closing the chapter I want to note something else about him. After his amazing escape, everyone wanted to know why he had to interrupt the process of his escape as often as he did. Smiling, the magician admitted that he didn't *have* to interrupt the process. After all, his escape was based on knowledge. But he needed something in addition to knowledge. He needed enthusiasm. And when he would leap from the cabinet the applause of the crowd stirred up his enthusiasm.[4]

Double binds are powerful. They may seem to cuff you and lock you in a dark cabinet. Getting out involves knowledge. But you also need the help of other men to stoke your enthusiasm. When the odds are against you, the support of a friend or two might make the difference between slavery and freedom. And brother, your encouragement could make the same difference in one of your friends.

DISCUSSION QUESTIONS

1. What are the five characteristics of an authentic man?
2. How did Jesus demonstrate these?
3. Which of these characteristics do you find the hardest to build into your life?
4. How did Jesus respond to Peter, knowing that Peter had let him down?
5. Is there somebody who has disappointed you? Do you need to forgive him or her? If so, think through the steps you'll take in doing so.

CHAPTER 12

Thank God Almighty, I Am Free at Last

Early one morning, about 4:00 A.M., I woke up in a cold sweat and found myself full of despair and anger. I had just turned forty the week before. As a counselor, I know all of the implications of turning forty—in fact, I had helped many men deal with their mid-life transitions. But this time, *I* was going through it. I had probably lived more than half of my allotted time. Somehow I thought that knowing the implications and having counseled other men through this transition might spare me my own midlife crisis. It didn't.

So I began to reflect on my life. I had achieved most of my goals. I had a master's degree in theology from a top-notch seminary, where I had won the preaching award. I had a Ph.D. in marriage and family counseling. I was a licensed psychologist and a respected counselor in Colorado. I had written books, articles, and spoken to thousands of people at conferences and seminars. I had traveled around the world and was a tenured professor at a very good seminary. I have a wonderful wife. I now work for the fastest-growing Christian organization ever in Christendom—Promise Keepers. So what is the big deal? Everything is great. Right?

Like many other men, I climbed the ladder in my areas of specialization, and when I got to the top I found that the ladder was leaning against the wrong wall. I looked inside and found that in spite of my accomplishments I felt empty. I felt like the older brother in the parable of the Prodigal Son. When the prodigal son returned home, the father threw a party for him just because he was home. His older brother, however, was mad because he himself had stayed home and had been obedient, but his dad hadn't thrown a party for him. In the story the older brother points out that he had been a good son; he was always there—always performing—yet why hadn't Dad ever thrown a party for him? Do you remember what his father said? "My child, you have always been with me, and all that is mine is yours." The father was pointing out that he had always been available for his son, the older son had always been too busy performing to enjoy the relationship.

I felt like that older brother. I had obeyed all the rules and had done everything right. I had not gotten into trouble and I had been the good son—always performing. So why wasn't I experiencing the abundant life? Why wasn't I having fun? I deserved it. I had earned it. Right? *Wrong!* Even in my own ministry, I discovered, I had defined myself by who I knew, what I did, and what I owned. All the while, the Father was there saying, "My child, I am here." But I was too busy performing.

Jesus said, "A thief comes only to steal and kill and destroy; I have come that they may have life, and have it to the full" (John 10:10).

So what *is* this abundant life Jesus speaks of? I thought I was living it, but if so, why did I feel so empty?

Men have been robbed. The thief has come to steal, to kill, and to destroy. The thief is the Devil and his world system. His job is to do whatever he can to keep us distracted from our true purpose for being here, which is to "glorify God and enjoy him forever" (Westminster Catechism). The thief has stolen the true meaning of life and in the end we begin to believe the phrase Burt Reynolds coined, "Life is hard—and then you die." When the thief steals a man's purpose, he has killed and destroyed him. Life becomes relegated to a "here and now" philosophy. But it doesn't have to be that way. There is an alternative.

Jesus said, "I have come that they may have life, and have it to the full." Some translations say, ". . . and have it more abundantly." The word "abundant" in this context means living life to its fullest. Jesus came to rescue us from the thief and to return to us the purpose for which we have been called—to be in relationship with him.

When I was growing up on the farm in Ohio, I remember asking my dad some important questions—well, important to a seven-year-old. "Daddy," I said, "why do geese fly south in the winter and come back in the spring? And why do all the pigs and cows seem to have babies in the spring and not at other times?"

My dad, who was a patient man, thought for a moment and then answered. "Well, son, God has placed something inside each animal called instinct. This tells them what to do and when to do it. It guides their lives."

I was satisfied with the answer, but then Dad asked me a question. "Son, have you ever noticed people? With all of their potential, they don't seem to know what they are doing or where they are going."

"Yeah, why is that?" I asked.

"Because God has placed within every person an empty space that only he can fill. God wants to be our director—God wants to be our guide. And when a person invites God into his life, he now knows what to do and where to go—because he knows *whose* he is."

Living without Christ is like driving a car with its front end out of alignment. You can stay on the road only by gripping the steering wheel with both hands and hanging on tightly. Any distraction, however, and you head straight for the ditch. Coming to Christ is a little like getting a front-end alignment. This is not to say there won't be bumps and potholes ahead that try to jar us off the road. Temptations and challenges will always test our alertness. But the basic skew in the moral mechanism has been repaired. "Therefore, if any one is in Christ, he is a new creation; the old has gone, the new has come!" (2 Cor. 5:17).

Abundant Life—true freedom—is when we fulfill the purpose for which we have been designed. A man who is free—who has escaped the double binds—knows that "whose he is" determines what he does. Jesus said in Mark 8:36, "If anyone would come after me, he must deny himself and take up his cross and follow me. For whoever wants to save his life shall lose it, but whoever loses his life for me and for the gospel will save it. What good is it for a man to gain the whole world, yet forfeit his soul? Or what can a man give in exchange for his soul?" Freedom is simply this: letting Jesus lead.

But how do we stay focused on *whose* we are rather than on *what* we do?

STAYING IN POSITION

In the fall, there is nothing I enjoy more than watching a good football game. In fact, I have a routine I go through when I arrive home just before a game is about to start. I throw my hat into the closet, go downstairs to our recreation room, and settle into my big blue leather recliner with a bowl of popcorn and some iced tea.

One night, as I settled down to watch the Denver Broncos play the Raiders, I noticed that something was not quite right. There was a lot of snow in the picture. Although I could see figures moving on the screen, I could not tell one team from the other or who had the ball. There was a lot of background noise, and the commentators' voices were garbled and cracked. I knew if I was going to enjoy this game, I would have to solve the problem. Assessing the situation, I noticed that the antennae were out of position for that particular station. So I adjusted the rabbit ears and there it was: a clear, crisp, beautiful picture. The colors were so bright, they practically shouted at me. I could see the orange and blue uniforms of the Broncos and the silver and black of the Raiders. Then the commentators' voices were clear. I could now enjoy the game—all because of some simple adjustments.

Similarly, if you and I are not continually making sure our spiritual antennae are in the right position we can pick up the wrong signals and even get the wrong picture. If we are to be free men, we must make sure we stay in the right position. How? How do we stay focused so we stay free?

Jesus gives us his four-part formula in John 15:1–15, in a passage that is part of the so-called "Upper Room Discourse" (John 13–17). This particular discourse is extremely important because at this particular point in Christ's life, he has less than twenty hours before being hung on a cross and placed in a tomb. Jesus had already given the disciples their purpose statement for their ministry, but he also knew they would face major challenges that could get them off track. So he gives them these four pieces of advice for staying focused.

Part One: Abide

In John 15:4–9 (RSV), Jesus uses the word *abide* no less than eight times:

> Abide in me, and I in you. As the branch cannot bear fruit by itself, unless it abides in the vine, neither can you, unless you abide in me. I am the vine, you are the branches. He who abides in me, and I in him, he it is that bears much fruit, for apart from me you can do nothing. If a man does not abide in me, he is cast forth as a branch and withers; and the branches are gathered, thrown into the fire and burned.

> If you abide in me, and my words abide in you, ask whatever you will, and it shall be done for you. By this my Father is glorified, that you bear much fruit, and so prove to be my disciples. As the Father has loved me, so have I loved you; abide in my love.

The word *abide* means, "to live in—as in a house; to dwell in—as in a residence. A place of sustenance and refuge." If we are to keep focused on our purpose in life, we must abide in him. In verses 4–5, Jesus points out that to try to stay focused apart from abiding in him would be like a branch trying to bear fruit apart from the vine. It is impossible.

Whenever I think of abiding, I think of a scene from the movie *2010,* in which the Russian cosmonaut and the American engineer must leave the Russian spaceship and go over to the American ship. In order to get there, however, they have to execute a lengthy space walk with only a "lifeline" hooked between them. The Russian had a power pack to keep him on course, but the American—on the other end of the lifeline—was totally dependent on the Russian cosmonaut's direction and power pack. The American astronaut knew that if the lifeline was cut, he would be swallowed up by the hostile environment around them. His life depended on that line.

Similarly, every day, you and I step out into a hostile environment. Jesus says in verses 18–19 of John 15 that the society in which we live threatens our values, our families, and yes, our very being. Yet we can go into this environment with confidence because our lifeline to Jesus can never be broken. Better yet, when we start going off course, we have a power pack—Jesus is the believer's power pack. When we get overwhelmed, we can call on him and he will give us the power we need to stay on course. I have discovered that when all you have is God—God is enough. A man who *abides* in Jesus can stay free from the double binds of life.

Part Two: Obedience

You may say, "That's great, Rod, but how do I keep abiding?" Jesus gives us the next part of the formula in John 15:10–11 (RSV):

> If you keep my commandments, you will abide in my love, just as I have kept my Father's commandments and abide in his love. These things I have spoken to you, that my joy may be in you, and that your joy may be full.

In these verses, Jesus shows us that *obedience* (that is, keeping God's commandments) is the key for abiding in him. Jesus said that his mission was to do the Father's will. Obeying the Father brought Jesus joy—and yet, this type of obedience seems rare today. Chuck Swindoll says in his book *Seasons of Life* that

> there's a strange species of Christian running loose today. . . . Who are they? They are the ones who rewrite the Bible to accommodate their lifestyle. We've all met them. From the skin out they have all of the appearance of your basic believer, but down inside, operation

rationalization transpires daily. They are experts at rephrasing or explaining away the painful truth of the text.

How do they think? Well, it's not very complicated. Whenever they run across Scripture verses or principles that attack their position, they alter them to accommodate their practice. That way, two things occur:

1. All desires (no matter how wrong) are fulfilled.
2. All guilt (no matter how justified) is erased.

That way, everybody can do his own thing and nobody has any reason to question anybody's action. If he does, call him a "legalist" and plow right on. Oh, yeah, you've gotta talk a lot about grace, too. That helps spook the bunch who would otherwise criticize.[1]

Let me give you some examples. As a counselor, I hear all kinds of "reasons" for doing things that are clearly disobedient, like, "I know God wants me to be happy. I can't stay married to her. She's just not supportive. God wants me to have someone who will support me." Or how about this one: "Look, I admit I should have been more honest on my tax return. But, hey, if I can save a little money, that's more for God, right?"

Wrong! I have found that convenient obedience is not really obedience at all. If we are going to abide in him we must be obedient—even it is inconvenient.

Coach McCartney tells of the story about a man who came to one of our Promise Keepers conferences. This man had lost thirty thousand dollars in a business deal with a friend. He was bitter and angry but asked God to forgive him for his bitterness and to forgive the man who had, in essence, stolen his thirty thousand dollars. He did not know that at another Promise Keepers conference, the man who had taken his money had been convicted of his wrongdoing and realized that he must be obedient and make restitution.

The man who had stolen the thirty thousand dollars contacted his former friend, asked for forgiveness, and paid him back in full. Now both men had peace of mind because of their obedience to God.

Obedience to Christ's commands keeps us focused on what is important and keeps us from yielding to what is urgent.

But how does one have that type of "want to" obedience?

Part Three: Loving

Notice the progression in Jesus' four-part formula. First, to stay focused, one must *abide*, but to abide, one must *obey*. But in order to obey, Jesus gives us the third part of the formula in verses 12–13 of John 15 (RSV): we must *love*.

> This is my commandment, that you love one another as I have loved you. Greater love has no man than this, that a man lay down his life for his friends.

That's not just any kind of love. It must be agape love, which is unconditional, accepting, and available. This is not the kind of love the world gives. In fact, our consistent love for God and one another will be a clear picture to those around us that something is different about our purpose and our values in life. In these verses, however, Jesus also implies that if my love is inconsistent with him, it will be inconsistent with everyone's because my love for others is a direct reflection of my love for God.

Have you ever felt overwhelmed by the command to love unconditionally? When men ask me, "How can I start being a loving person?" I give the same answer I give to those who ask how they can start jogging: Start slow—and then get slower! For the first week, the goal is to just keep running. Too many men buy new shoes and a fancy running suit, and then sprint out the door, eagerly chugging as hard as they can for about three blocks. Then their stomachs begin to ache, their muscles cramp, and their lungs burn. (Sound familiar?) They wind up hitchhiking home, exhausted and gasping, "I'll never do that again!" That is called anaerobic (without oxygen) running because the body is using up more oxygen than it takes in.

Many men run that way, and many love that way too. They love with great fervor and self-sacrifice, giving 100 percent, but without the resources to make it last for a lifetime. Down the road they find themselves in pain, gasping and cramped, saying, "I'll never do that again."

Love, like running, must be aerobic. Our output must be matched by our intake. Running requires oxygen. An enduring love requires God's Word, his consolation, his presence. As we love aerobically, we'll build up our capacity to do more and more. And pretty soon we won't be huffing and puffing before the first half mile—we'll be running marathons.

But there is a fourth part. In order for a man to stay focused he must *abide;* to abide he must *obey;* to obey he must *love;* and to love, a man needs something more.

Part Four: Knowing

Finally, in John 15:14–15 (RSV), Jesus describes the key to being a loving person. It is knowing him.

> You are my friend if you do what I command you. No longer
> I call you servants, for the servant does not know what the master
> is doing; but I have called you friends, for all that I have heard
> from my Father I have made known to you.

Notice what Jesus calls the disciples: his "friends." Did you catch that? *What* does it mean to be friends with somebody? A friend is someone I can count on—someone I can share my deepest thoughts with and still be accepted—someone who likes me in spite of myself. But how do you get to *know* someone? I believe there are three ingredients:

1. *Spend time with him.* At Dallas Seminary I was blessed to have some good friends. We would meet weekly for Bible study and prayer. We lived in the same dorm, we ate together, and we really got to know each other. I knew their hearts and their struggles. And they got to know mine. By spending time with each other, we got to *know* each other. Their hurts became my hurts—their joys, my joys.

That is the kind of friendship the Lord wants with us. Are you getting consistent time with the Lord? I do not ask this question to lay a guilt trip on you, for I struggle with this myself, but I have learned that when I fail to spend regular time with God, then I begin to lose my focus and his heart ceases to be my heart.

2. *Talk.* When I was dating my wife, we would spend hours talking on the phone. Before we got married, we really wanted to learn about each other. There was a sense of wonderment about the other person, and I learned so much about my future wife that was exciting. Through talking, her heart became my heart, her desires became my desires, and vice versa.

But once we lose that sense of wonderment about another person, we cease to talk to them. We lose the "heartbeat" of the other person, and the relationship begins to die. Studies indicate that most husbands and wives spend less than thirty minutes a week in meaningful conversation.

So how are you doing in the area of talking to God? Yes, I am talking about prayer. It is through my talking to God and listening to what he has to say that his heartbeat becomes mine and his focus, my focus. If communication is the life blood of a relationship, I must make sure God and I communicate regularly.

3. *Be transparent.* The third key to knowing someone is to be transparent with them. It is only through being open, honest, and vulnerable with others that intimacy can take place.

I remember one summer when I was really struggling with lust— yep, lust. It was a hot summer, and it seemed that everywhere I looked, the women were wearing less and less and I was seeing more and more. Now, don't get me wrong. I have a good marriage. But as a *man,* I was having lust attacks. So I sat down with an older male friend and shared with him my struggles in this area. Since he was seventy years old, I figured he had probably overcome this problem long ago. So I asked him at what age a man begins to get over his lustful feelings.

With a straight face he told me, "Seventy-one. Ask me next year, and I'll say seventy-two." He then shared with me how he also struggled in this area. We made a pact to continue to pray for one another and also made an agreement that we would do two things: first, we would thank God he had given us passion and desire; and second, we would pray for the women we were lusting after, knowing that they were children of God. This really cut down on the lustful thoughts. It was through such transparency that we got to know each other.

Are you transparent with God? Do you share with him your fears, lusts, failures, and even anger at him? Yes, anger at him. You get mad at your friends, don't you? I know I do. When I feel betrayed or misunderstood, I tell them. We remain friends after the conflict because that is what friends do. And so it is with God. I get angry with him and, at times, feel forsaken by him.

In many of his psalms, David would say, "But still I trust in God." In the Garden of Gethsemane Jesus was transparent. He told God that he wanted to find a way out of having to die, but in the end Jesus made it clear that it was not his will but the Father's that was important. Jesus was transparent.

Men, be open with God. He can handle whatever you throw at him. He will not reject you—you are his sons. When we are open to the Lord, we can then be open with one another. Remember, you have nothing to prove, nothing to lose, and nothing to hide.

How do we stay free from the double binds? *Abide—obey— love—and know him.*

Recently, as I flew to Los Angeles for a speaking engagement, I overheard the pilot mention that our landing would be free of human guidance. It was done totally by computers. The pilot said that as the plane makes its descent, the tower would send out a "true beam" from their computer. The pilot would then turn on the computer on his instrument panel. The tower would then say, "Okay, thirty degrees right—now twenty degrees left. Okay, let go of the controls. You are now locked onto the true beam." Once locked onto the beam, the tower's computer can bring planes in for an accurate, safe landing.

Every day as a man, we navigate some pretty tough societal head winds. There are times when we drift thirty degrees to the right or twenty degrees to the left. But we also have a true beam—his name is Jesus Christ. When we listen for his instructions and let him lock onto our internal computer—the heart—he will bring us in for a safe landing every time.

DISCUSSION QUESTIONS

1. Name the key distracters that get you "out of position" with the Lord. Which one needs the most work? Start this week with that one.
2. Time-Talk-Transparency are what help us to stay "intimate" with the Lord. Which is your strongest and why? Which one is your weakest? How will you begin to change in that area?
3. Spend some time thanking God that even though we may let go at times—he doesn't.

Notes

Chapter 1. Double Trouble

1. Marvin Allen with Jo Robinson, *Angry Men—Passive Men* (New York: Fawcett Columbine, 1993), 26.

2. Sam Keen and Ofer Zur, *Psychology Today* (March 1989), results printed in *Psychology Today* (November 1989).

3. Fred Hayward, "Men as Success Objects," *UTNE Reader* no. 81 (May–June 1991), 81. Excerpted from *Family Networker* magazine (November–December 1988).

4. Aaron R. Kipnis, *Knights Without Honor* (New York: Tarcher/Putnam, 1993), 41.

Chapter 2. Escape to Freedom

1. Herbert Goldberg, *The New Male: From Self-Destruction to Self-Care* (New York: William Morrow, 1979), 13.

2. David Needham, *Birthright* (Portland: Multnomah, 1979).

Chapter 3. A Man's Gotta Do What a Man's Gotta Do

1. Greg Howard and Craig Macintosh, "Sally Forth" cartoon strip, *Denver Post* (April 18–21, 1995).

2. James Moore, *Self-Image* (Institute of Biblical Counseling Discussion Guide—Colorado Springs: NavPress, 1992).

3. Harry Levinson, "On Executive Suicide," *Harvard Business Review,* vol. 53, no. 4 (July–August 1975), 118.

4. Goldberg, *The New Male,* 50.

5. Brennan Manning, *Abba's Child* (Colorado Springs: NavPress, 1994), 61, 78.

6. Eugene Peterson, *The Message* (Colorado Springs: NavPress, 1994).

Chapter 4. I Owe, I Owe, So Off to Work I Go

1. Gordon Dahl, *Work, Play and Worship in a Leisure-Oriented Society* (Minneapolis: Augsburg, 1972), 12.

2. Sam Keen, *Fire in the Belly* (New York: Bantam, 1991), 51–52.

3. Warren Farrel excerpted from *The Family Networker* (November–December 1988).

4. Ted Dobson: quote from a class lecture.

5. Robert Hemfelt, Frank Minirth, and Paul Meier, *We Are Driven* (Nashville: Oliver Nelson, 1995), 21–22.

6. Samuel Osherson, "Finding Our Fathers," quoted in David Stoop and Stephen Arterburn, *The Angry Man* (Dallas: Word, 1991).

7. Anonymous prayer quoted in Tim Hansel, *When I Relax I Feel Guilty* (Elgin, Ill.: David C. Cook, 1979).

Chapter 5. No Fear

1. Kipnis, *Knights Without Honor,* 21.

2. Stu Weber, *Tender Warrior* (Portland: Multnomah, 1993), 41.

3. Warren Farrel, *The Myth of Male Power* (New York: Simon and Schuster, 1993), 106.

4. Joe Bailey

Chapter 6. What's Going On in There Anyway?

1. Goldberg, *The New Male,* 23.

2. John Gray, *Men Are from Mars and Women Are from Venus* (New York: HarperCollins, 1992), 17.

3. Patrick Morley, *The Seven Seasons of a Man's Life* (Nashville: Thomas Nelson, 1995), 21.

4. Goldberg, *The New Male*, 23–24.

5. Larry Letich, "Do You Know Who Your Friends Are?" *UTNE Reader* (May–June 1991).

6. Ivan Maisel, *Dallas Morning Herald* (August 4, 1992).

Chapter 7. I'm Just A-Passin' Through

1. Source unknown.

2. Quote by Max Anders from E. Glenn Wagner, *The Awesome Power of Shared Belief* (Dallas: Word, 1995), 77.

3. Morley, *The Seven Seasons*, 144.

Chapter 8. Hit the Road, Jack

1. The anecdote about Viktor Frankl is from Allen Klein, *The Healing Power of Humor* (New York: Putnam, 1989), xxii.

2. Charles Swindoll, *Seasons of Life* (Portland: Multnomah, 1983), 100.

3. Quote from Saint-Exupéry is from Jack Canfield and Mark Victor Hansen, *Chicken Soup for the Soul* (Florida: Health Communications, Inc., 1993), 37–39.

Chapter 9. Tender and Tough

1. Walter Trobisch, *All a Man Can Be and What Every Woman Should Know* (Downers Grove, Ill.: InterVarsity, 1983), 75.

2. Ibid., 80.

3. Canfield and Hansen, *Chicken Soup for the Soul*, 12.

4. Trobisch, *All a Man Can Be*, 635.

5. David G. Meyers, *The Human Puzzle* (New York: Harper & Row, 1978), 147.

Chapter 10: The Peaceful Man

1. Trobisch, *All a Man Can Be*, 85–93.

2. Stanley C. Baldwin, *Bruised But Not Broken* (Portland: Multnomah Press, 1985), 20–21.

Chapter 11. The Authentic Man

1. This story is related in Charles Swindoll, *Come Before Winter* (Portland: Multnomah Press, 1985), 283–84.

2. Larry Crabb, *The Marriage Builder* (Grand Rapids: Zondervan, 1992), 34–35.

3. Alan Loy McGinnis, *The Friendship Factor* (Minneapolis: Augsburg, 1979), 36.

4. Swindoll, *Come Before Winter*, 284.

Chapter 12. Thank God Almighty, I Am Free at Last

1. Swindoll, *Seasons of Life*, 244–45.